AYLESBURY

A Personal Memoir from the 1920s

The ruins of St Peter's Church at Quarrendon from a photograph pre-1905.
By the 1920s there are clear memories of only one remaining arch, the entire
site being overgrown with wild roses, brambles and nettles. Buckinghamshire
County Museum image reference AYBLM Quarrendon I (Reproduced by
kind permission of the Museum).

W. R. MEAD

Aylesbury

A Personal Memoir from the 1920s

with
Original Drawings by
Douglas Carter

Pensez, c'est vivre:
Se souvenir, c'est revivre

PUBLISHED BY THE AUTHOR

First published in the United Kingdom 1996 by
W. R. Mead
6 Lower Icknield Way
Aston Clinton
Nr Aylesbury, Buckinghamshire
HP22 5JS

This revised and expanded edition published 2009

A catalogue record for this book is available from the British Library.

ISBN 978-1-902613-06-2

Designed and typeset in Monotype Bembo by Discript Limited, London WC2N 4BN
Printed in the United Kingdom by Athenæum Press, Gateshead

*Dedicated to the memory of
my brother and to all those friends
with whom we shared schooldays in
Aylesbury in the 1920s.*

CONTENTS

ILLUSTRATIONS

Most of the illustrations have been drawn – most of them especially for this memoir – by Douglas Carter, very much a kindred spirit to whom I am much indebted. The maps are reproduced by permission of the Ordnance Survey.

PREFACE

This personal memoir has been prompted by the appearance of a number of publications – a book of old photographs of Aylesbury gleaned by Elliot Viney and Pamela Nightingale, *The Book of Aylesbury* (1994) by Clive Birch, *The Pictoral History of Aylesbury* (1993) by Julian Hunt and Hugh Hanley and a sprinkling of reminiscences by Aylesburians in the magazine of the Aylesbury Society. When two or three old inhabitants came together, chatter about former times often takes over the conversation. It is an integral part of the process of what Pablo Picasso called "growing young". For some time past, it has seemed to me a great pity not to record the recollections that friendly gatherings have stirred. At least this will give a somewhat longer life to memories which have become a part of social history.

It is not easy to grasp the reality of a time from which one is long removed. It might have sharpened the memory to turn the pages of *The Bucks Herald* or to have added to the detail of homes and their occupants by looking through the relevant volume of *Kelly's Directory*. Both sources have been deliberately avoided because to have consulted them would have been to change the character of what follows. No attempt is made to produce a complete picture. Only the people and places that have left a personal impression have been included – people, discriminatingly: places, less so. Others will remember different places, different faces, different scenes and will recall them in a different perspective.

Here and there, questions asked at the time and the replies received of elders and betters are remembered. (They have been included in brackets). No attempt is made to compare the past and present and indulgence in the wisdom of hindsight is reduced to a minimum. Let the words of Charles Baudelaire be all that is said of nostalgia –

> . . . *la forme d'une ville*
> *Change plus vite, hélas, que la cœur d'un mortel.*

December 1995

This memoir, published privately for friends in the first instance, rapidly ran out of print. Second hand copies have regularly been sought. Since 1995, other memoirs, picture books and historical studies of Aylesbury have multiplied and a special edition of the Ordnance Survey map of 1923 (with an introduction by Julian Hunt) has been published. New insights into the setting of Aylesbury in the Vale have been given in the greatly appreciated text of Kenneth and Margaret Morley – "'Tis the Fair Famous Vale" (2007).

This second edition of the memoir has been considerably extended and it also includes what can only be called some autobiographical indulgences referring to school days. There is also a section on Notes relating to specific items in the text as well as a short appendix.

During the past decade, changes in the form and character of Aylesbury have been greatly speeded up. They bring to mind the appealing antithesis of Jonathan Sachs between the "ephemeral now" and the "eternal then". Just occasionally something of the "eternal then" can be recaptured in what local estate agents call Old Aylesbury. Charter day can also open up glimpses of the living past.

And so can the lively sketches of Nick Carter. No one has quite captured with his line drawings the "spirit of Aylesbury past". The sketches that he drew especially for the 1995 edition have been supplemented with a few that recall his Christmas cards. It is typical of him that he should have handed the copyright on his drawings to the Aylesbury Society. I am grateful to Roger King for permission to reproduce the drawings of Parson's Fee, St Osyth's and the Market Square.

Acknowledgement must be made first to Linda Bomken. Over the last decade she has dealt with many of my manuscripts, but for several reasons none has called for more patience than this. I am greatly indebted to her for her professionalism and forbearance. The technical assistance of Anita Youkee has also been much appreciated. The ammonites on the cover design commemorate a photographic foray by Bill Willett of those in the walls around Hartwell park. For permission to reproduce the colourful finial on the back cover and the photograph of the ruins of St Peter's Church at Quarrendon, I am grateful to the Buckinghamshire County Museum. The illustration of the plant named after Richard Mead (p.91) is reproduced by the kind permission of the Director and the Board of trustees, Royal Botanic Gardens, Kew. The Aylesbury maps are reproduced by permission of the Ordnance Survey. Finally – and once again – it has been a pleasure to have had the professional expertise and guidance of Richard Bates in dealing with the manuscript – not forgetting the pleasure of working again in his bijou premises in Bedfordbury, Covent Garden.

W. R. Mead
January 2009

I

"A LOCAL HABITATION AND A NAME"

This is a brief chronicle of Aylesbury as it appeared in the middle 1920s in my early schooldays. It is a view of the town and the surrounding countryside compiled from what might be called "naïve knowledge" unwittingly absorbed. There is no accounting for the things that stick in the mind and those that are forgotten. "Life's an affair of instants", wrote John Masefield. At some instant, lasting impressions were made of the streets, the façades of their buildings and the faces of the people who lived behind them.

Aylesbury in the mid 1920s was a modest county town. The phrase "The Vale of Aylesbury" sounded pleasant on the ear. In print, the name Aylesbury looked strange to a schoolboy. At first it was hard to spell. Nor was it at all easy to pronounce, even by those born with the Bucks dialect. Aylesbury had a population of about 12,000. It was located upon a hill. The hill was not especially pronounced. Nevertheless, except when coming from Bierton, its inclines made the elderly puff and caused the cyclists to stretch their muscles. Within the town, all references to direction were given in terms of "up" and "down".

Aylesbury was a brick and slate town. There were plenty of small brickyards in the neighbourhood, but the slate must have had to wait the coming of the railway age. The paving stones, the granite setts and kerbstones which gleamed in the sunshine after rain, were also foreign features. Aylesbury was a compact town with no more than a little straggling housing development down the country roads. Ribbon development proper had not yet begun. New features called "council houses" were just appearing, with Southcourt a pioneering estate. Even in the town, many houses had front gardens, albeit handkerchief in size. They were entered by a gate and often had iron railings. The railings made a sequence of musical sounds if you struck them with a stick as you passed by.

Everything about the town was on a small scale. Most people walked to work: shopping was done on foot. The pace of life was

slow. Everybody seemed to know or to know of everybody else
– everybody else's business, too. Most residents had country roots.
Immigrants were "foreigners". Houses were sold for hundreds rather
than thousands of pounds. Something called "rates" were spoken
of and the adjective "high" was regularly applied to them.
Parsimony was favoured by those who paid them. Perhaps, for this
reason, Aylesbury was a town not given to elaborate street
furnishings. Statuary was minimal save for that given by private
individuals – hence John Hampden, Lord Chesham with his lions,
and Benjamin Disraeli. Fountains were absent save for a waterless
feature in Kingsbury Square and an empty drinking trough in the
Market Square. Street lighting was economical; public seats and
benches, rare. There was a rather mean grassy area called "The
Recreation Ground". There were no parks and gardens. As a boy,
one looked in vain for the "park" in Queen's Park, Victoria Park
and Manor Park.

Businesses were on a small scale and most were family-owned.
The words "Ltd." or "And C°." were exceptional, though it was
known that the Co-operative store (which accepted things called
"token coins") fell into a strangely different category. Most shops
opened at eight o'clock in the morning and closed at six o'clock
in the evening – later on Saturdays. Thursday was early closing
day with a total shut down at one o'clock. Shops also closed for
an hour in the middle of the day. Factory hooters sounded at
twelve noon, the morning shift having begun at seven o'clock.
Streams of cycles emerged from factories and workshops bearing
those who went home for lunch. Some cyclists carried colleagues
on their "cross bars" – even on their "pillion" seat. The few ladies
who cycled still wore skirts. A network of strings from the back
mudguard to the hub of the wheel prevented skirts from catching
in the spokes of the wheel. Motorcyclists with side-cars, cumbersome delivery lorries and pot-holed mid-town roads were the
principal hazards for the cyclists of the day. The hooter sounded
for the return to work at one o'clock and again at six o'clock, at
the end of the working day.

Commercial competition was on a small scale, but fairly intense.
There were six "family" grocers within half a mile of each other.

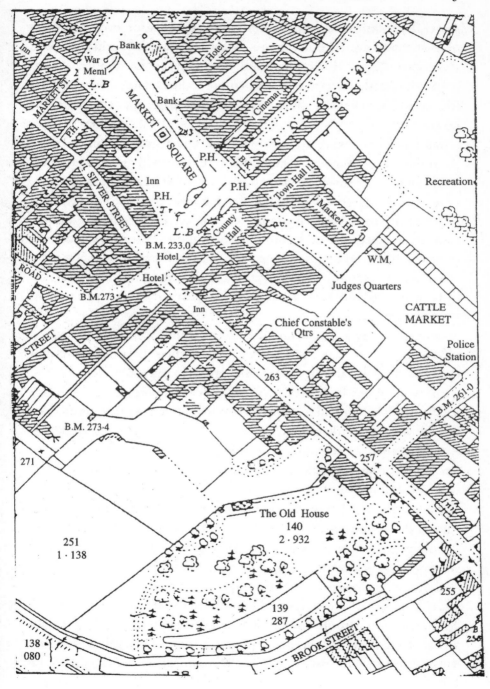

Fig. 1. A map of the centre of Aylesbury (reproduced from the 1925 OS Map).

An equal number of greengrocers suffered the additional competition of the cheap fruit and vegetables of the twice-weekly market. Bakers, butchers, newsagents and confectioners were even more numerous. There were half a dozen coal merchants. None of the four or five jewellers, clock and watch repairers seemed to lack business.

All customers expected personal delivery of goods – and usually at times to suit their convenience. Consequently, the trading community employed an army of delivery men and errand boys. Once a "delivery boy" always a "delivery boy" it seemed, for some were well past boyhood. Goods were carried on heavily framed bicycles. On dark winter evenings, oil lamps marked their presence. The weak flames were easily extinguished by the wind.

Goods also came by hand cart, by horse-drawn delivery van, by milk float, by butcher's dray and by coal cart. The motor lorry seemed only to be used to collect rubbish, which was rarely contained in any kind of bin. Where it was dumped no one seemed to know or to care. The railways had their own horse-drawn delivery service. Street sweepers pushed three-wheeled trucks. Chimney sweeps had their own barrows. (Did one have a donkey and cart?) The post office provided uniformed telegram boys with red bicycles. Postmen, with their big canvas bags (reputed to be made by men in prison), came mostly on foot. There seemed to be letter boxes everywhere; many were built into walls. The occasional knifegrinder and scissors sharpener, rotating his grindstone with a pedal, moved from street to street. The rag and bone man still shouted his trade. Sandwich men (a name which intrigued children) carried their billboards on market days. More rarely, a hurdy-gurdy man with his barrel organ appeared.

Among the noises that still linger in the ear are the bells of St Mary's church. They chimed every half hour day and night. Enthusiastic bell ringers assembled at every opportunity, especially for weddings, when generous quantities of rice as well as confetti were thrown. The three bells of Walton parish church could be heard when the wind blew from the south. They rang with greater urgency than those of St Mary's. The bells of Bierton church could be heard when the wind was in the north. The Market

Square clock struck a rather second-rate note. Half a dozen hooters sounded and the whistle of departing trains blew regularly. Bicycle bells tinkled; motor horns sounded raucously when they did not toot. When a fire was reported, a hooter sounded. Its purpose was to call together a fire brigade which consisted mostly of paid volunteers. The fire bell clanged as the engine rushed to the site of the outbreak. And there were humbler sounds. Early morning cocks crowed from kitchen gardens in the middle of the town. One dog's bark might set another dozen responding to disturb the night-time silence.

In an Aylesbury which was smaller and leafier, the sounds of nature were still common. Owls were to be heard regularly. There were plenty of friendly blackbirds and sparrows around in winter. Nor was it unusual for a robin to appear at a back door in the middle of town. Caged birds were common canaries and budgerigars were given a daily airing in their cages outside homes in the town. Two raucous parrots were to be heard in the vicinity of Buckingham Street.

In the large walled garden of the Locke family, there were beehives. There is a memory of a queen bee attracting a swarm in Buckingham Street and an apparition in white proceeding on the pavement, empty hive in hand, in pursuit of a free swarm of honey bees.

There were mysteries which puzzled a child. Telephone lines hummed on the top of sturdy brown poles. (Was the humming the sound of conversations passing through them?) Water pipes threaded the streets. (Where did they come from?) Sometimes they burst in the road. What happened to the water that went down the sink, the bath, the drains in the street, the lavatory? It was reported that it went to a place down Bicester Road. Here were the so-called "roundabouts" that were the outward and visible signs of the sewage disposal plant, a place which was approached by a clinker lane and was out-of-bounds. There were also exciting legends of underground passages that burrowed their way from The King's Head to the church, but no one had personal experience of them. The gas pipes that threaded the town were being slowly replaced by electric cables. There were also sinister features called "rat runs".

The town had familiar smells. That of leaking gas was not unusual. Petrol fumes were of little concern. Momentary exhaust fumes yielded a cloud of blue smoke. ("Hold your nose until it blows away.") The faint smell of naphtha issued from bicycle lamps. In summer, there was the strong smell of tar and the hot smell of steam rollers as they puffed and clanked over the tar macadam, the granite chips of which crunched for weeks afterwards. Cyclists hated them: punctures multiplied. In winter, especially when the wind was gusty the smell of smoke was everywhere, because almost every house had open fires. The miscellany of chimney pots of every shape and size emitted smokes of various colours. When they caught fire, they yielded a strong sooty smell. Darker smoke hung above factory chimneys. It was taken for granted. Even those whose laundry hung in the immediate vicinity knew that complaint was useless. In frosty weather plumes of steam and smoke rose from railway engines. The north wind also brought in the smell of the brickworks from twenty miles away.

Games were played in the streets. No one objected, not even the passing policeman. In dry weather, frames for hop scotch were marked in chalk on the roads and pavements and not only in the back streets. The courses to be hopped might be oblong or spiral in outline. If you were seen to hop on a line, you lost a turn and started again. If you hopped successfully to the centre of the spiral or to the end of the oblong and back, you claimed a personal panel in the frame on which you could rest both feet. Other players had to hop over it. Nonsense rhymes were chanted to see who should have the first innings. "Fists up!" –

> Ollika, bollika, sooka, sollika,
> Ollika, bollika, nod.

Were the lines of the hopscotch frames the reason that some children were mesmerised by the cracks between the sandstone paving slabs? It was not unusual to see children lagging behind their parents as they planted their feet safely within the confines of individual paving stones.

Cricket stumps were chalked on brick walls as well as the

outlines of tennis nets. Games were held up momentarily if a vehicle passed. Bigger children played "Hare and hounds". The hare had several minutes' start, chalk-marking his track at intervals, usually with red or blue arrows. The word *graffiti* had yet to appear. Chalk marks on pavements, roads or brick walls – a part of the social documentation of 1920s childhood – were soon washed away by rain.

Marbles clinked in gutters seasonally. Peg tops were whipped; iron hoops were trundled. Wooden scooters rattled over pavements. Skipping ropes were twirled. They were principally used by girls, taken to school and regularly used in the playground. Longer ropes were twirled by couples. A variety of skipping rhymes were also chanted. Occasional kites were flown in the fields beyond the railway. Following a snowfall, which brought most traffic to a standstill and closed the cattle market, wooden boxes were dragged around by small boys as sleighs. There was no shortage of boxes for most wholesalers delivered their goods in wooden packing crates.

For a child, Aylesbury appeared to be a big place: it seemed to take a long time to cover it on foot. Most residents regarded it as the centre of the universe. To use the title of a seventeenth-century Digger's pamphlet, the town was very much "A light shining in Buckinghamshire". Few, if any, saw it in the perspective of a pinpoint on a map.

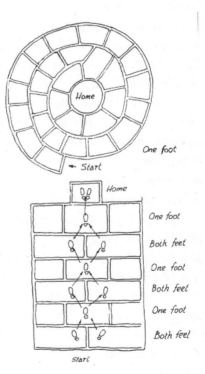

Fig. 2. Hop Scotch Frames

II

HOME TERRITORY

Since the birth certificate registered Buckingham Street, it is logical to survey the home territory from there. For some reason the eye turned first in the direction of Kingsbury, where there was a little cluster of shops that made an impression at an early age. "Comics" were bought from the newsagent's shop of Mrs Clarke and her daughter, Ida. The shop always seemed to have an odour of fried bacon, but for all her untidy hair, apron and carpet slippers, Mrs Clarke was bright-eyed and wonderfully friendly. Next door was Adams's, the tobacconists, with its contrasting scents. A carved wooden figure of a North American Indian stood outside the door. It was fascinating to see the loose tobacco being weighed on little brass scales and twisted up into paper packets. There were boxes of cigars, packets of cigarettes (some with exotic names such as *Abdullah*) and tins of snuff. Red polka-dot handkerchieves received the sneezes that it generated. Mrs Adams presided behind a glass-topped counter. She was a fount of local knowledge. A deaf-and-dumb son in the hairdressing parlour behind the shop cut boys' hair for sixpence and dispatched them with strongly-smelling hair spray. It was intriguing to watch him lip-reading as one sat on a stool in front of a large mirror.

Squeezed beside the tobacconist's shop was The Bonnet Box — probably one of the oldest houses in Kingsbury. Crouch's the jewellers shouldered it out of Buckingham Street. Miss Crouch had big pearly earrings and two Pekinese dogs on leads (Crouch was a name which set children giggling: likewise Tofield and Crump ... Why?) Cheerful Miss Hobley, hair-netted and with a large cameo brooch, had a window filled with jars of sweets. Pear drops, wine gums and violet cachous had little appeal. Humbugs, acid drops, licorice braid, coconut ice, sherbet dabs and gobstoppers were favoured. In summer, penny ice-cream cones were piled high with some kind of yellow frozen custard.

If you crossed the road at the corner of Kingsbury and Buckingham Street and climbed three stone steps, you came to the

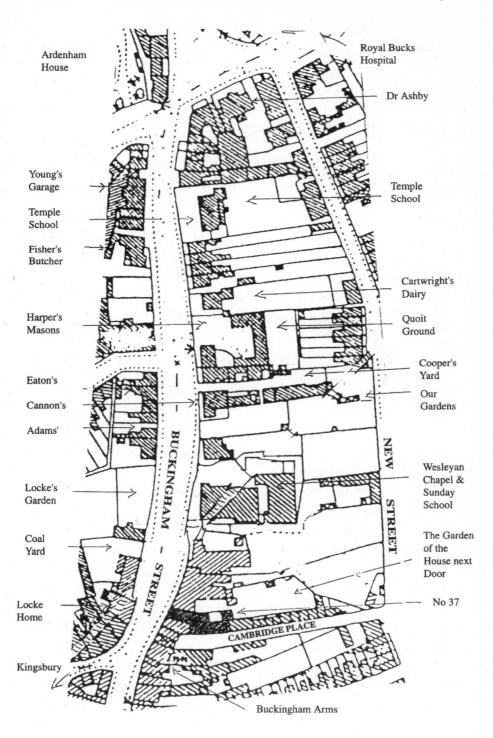

Fig. 3. A map of Buckingham Street (reproduced from the 1925 OS Map).

shop door (divided in two parts like that of a stable) of a baker. He was a fat baker, so too his wife and daughters. He and his family might have stepped straight out of the card game of Happy Families. He was a real life Mr Bun. The whole family had a smile for everyone and they were always willing to bake other people's Christmas and birthday cakes in their oven. They might even be persuaded to receive an earthen jar of jugged hare. Next door to the bakery and beside an arch leading to a secret garden, lived Mr Stanley Galpin, erstwhile organist at St Mary's church, with a brass plate announcing "Teacher of pianoforte". The shop of the adjacent saddlers and harnessmakers smelled of leather. It yielded to Mealin's bric-à-brac and second hand store with its miscellaneous wares overflowing on to the pavement. The somewhat neglected premises of the chain-smoking Mr Mealin sat a little incongruously beside Bedford House, the double-fronted house of the Locke family, which was the only house in the street that bore a name. Bedford House had a cottage extension on one side. Grey-bearded Alderman Locke had a pianist daughter. Her plaits were pinned ("like earphones" we used to say) on either side of her head. The piano came to life every morning with scales and exercises which filled the street, but were not exactly appreciated by near neighbours. Bedford House was next to a small wine and spirit store run by a tubby Mr Riley and his pretty bird-like wife. Behind these premises lay Locke's coal yard, complete with a stable for a draught horse and delivery wagon. The cart horse was a source of attraction, but the blackened men weighing and filling coal bags scared children away. So did Miss Locke as she moved around the walled garden with its lofty chestnut tree. For she kept bees and in her white beekeeper's outfit with a veiled hat, she presented a ghostly appearance. In one of the bay-windowed residences beyond the garden lived "Auntie Lily", whose elegant hats and white gloves never passed without notice when she went off on Sunday evenings to the Congregational church in High Street. (All chapels seemed to be called churches.) Her drop earrings also caused comment in days when to wear them was to have one's ears pierced (an operation which sounded rather dreadful to children). Mr Eaton, the compact, dark-moustached cabinet maker

– and funeral director – followed from the house next-door-but-one to add his mellifluous bass voice to the Congregational choir. His daughter Phyllis, with two plaits, was a "big" girl at Temple School. A rather desultory branch of the Co-op abutted on to Eaton's joinery workshop and faced the three-storeyed factory that was briefly a printing works. Beyond, was one of Aylesbury's many butchers – Albert Fisher, who had one attractive married daughter and one unmarried daughter who drove a pony and trap. Then came Young's garage, with its open charabancs for hire. A smaller general store plastered with cigarette advertisements and housing a cramped sub-post office, brought the properties to the junction of five roads.

Commanding this junction was the town's pride and joy – The Royal Buckinghamshire Hospital, with a bust of Florence Nightingale presiding over the entrance hall. Above were the prestigious Verney and Lee Wards, named after two county families. Opposite to the hospital and behind an incongruous clutter of billboards and down-at-heel stables stood an attractive house sheltered by high trees. It was Ardenham House, home of two sisters whose treble warblings at St Mary's church called forth suppressed mirth from nearby children. On the north side of the junction, adjacent to the disused Primitive Methodist Chapel, was the rather gloomy house of the big bluff Doctor Ashby.

Returning along the north side of Buckingham Street, the first impressive building was the Temple School for girls, junior boys and a handful of boarders. A notice, gold on black, indicated that it was run by the Misses Amery MA.LL.M. and Gleave. The four early Victorian houses next to Temple School are remembered because one was occupied by a dentist – "Not a fully qualified dentist because he is not allowed to give gas", it was said. But he was certainly allowed to undertake fillings. For this purpose he used a pedal-operated dental drill, the bands of which made a clicking noise when they rotated. The more frequent the clicks, the faster went the drill and the deeper the cavity became. More agreeable are the memories of the neighbouring handsome house. It was the residence of the Cartwrights who delivered milk. The daily milk round was made by pony and trap. In the trap were gleaming milk churns, together with quart, pint and half-pint measures. When the cry of the milkman (sometimes an attempted yodel, sometimes a refined war whoop) was heard, customers took out their jugs in readiness. Occasionally the milkman was accompanied by a girl with black curly hair.

Next door to the dairyman was Harper's, the monumental mason's. It is remembered for the chipping of the stone cutters and the whine of the stone-polishing machine which sent up a small cloud of dust. A pleasant double-fronted house was occupied by the family. It contrasted with the sombre looking neighbouring lodging house beside which opened a cul-de-sac — Cooper's Yard — harbouring two old cottages and several outbuildings. The cul-de-sac also led to the local quoits ground from which the clink of horse shoes could be heard as they struck each other in the grey muddy enclosure at which they were pitched. A handsome red brick house, always in perfect condition, lay on the other side of the cul-de-sac. It was a living advertisement for the firm of builders with which its owner was associated. The house was the home of Hattie Cannon — a most attractive person, pearled, carefully dressed, sometimes embarrassingly rouged. Her small spry husband, Leonard, had a pinched blue face. (He had reportedly been gassed during the war.) Memories of an impressive Wesleyan chapel are linked with the uncomfortable experience of being a page boy dressed in black satin at an aunt's wedding, with tales of an aged relative who had given a hundred pounds towards a new organ, and with tapping a foundation stone with a mallet — no doubt at a price — when the new Sunday school was built. The chapel was flanked by the manse on one side and by a small office building belonging to the district council. Thereafter, street numbers began to register with me.

Numbers 39–41 were occupied by the long double-fronted plate glass windows of the old-established furnishing business of the Jenns family. There was residential accommodation above and a large house behind, the latter possibly the oldest property on Buckingham Street. Number 37 bore the name of Boughton in the mosaic of the steps at the entrance. As with other shops, it had strange sockets at the edge of the pavement for poles to support

Fig. 4. No 37 Buckingham Street is the two-storeyed building on the right: 39–41 are adjacent. Two of the lime trees are shown.

the sun blinds which were used before the days of roller blinds. Number 35 was Peskitt's, a lady's dress shop. It was generous with haberdashery – cotton reels, mending wool, embroidery silks, hair pins, hat pins, slides and combs, hair nets and modesty vests, hooks and eyes, buttons and rolls of shining ribbons. Plater's men's outfitters, Number 33, had a range of fat pattern books dangling at the ready for made-to-measure suits. It was joined to *The Buckingham Arms*, about which hung an odour of stale beer, by a room over an archway. To the rear of *The Buckingham Arms*, there was stabling above which operated a deft basket-maker and repairer. His name was Piddington and he was not without musical interest ("Humerskew, my favourite piece"). Page's unrivalled bakery came next door, exuding the best of all possible smells. Cups, shields and silverware crowded the glass cases in the shop (with an equal number in cupboards beyond). One window was commonly occupied by a tiered wedding cake. The variety of fancy cakes – cream horns, cream donuts and buns, bridal slices, Battenburg slices – was unequalled. So, too, was the variety of bread. Wasps enjoyed a field day in the shop at high summer. Beyond the bakehouse, where mixing machines moaned from early in the morning, was Sale Brothers, another small family grocery store. The recently rebuilt The Two Brewers had a spacious yard regularly occupied by carrier's carts to which orders from the town's shops were delivered for transport to the surrounding villages. As was the case with several hostelries, market day lunches were advertised – "Roast and two vegetables". Sale's double-fronted picture shop adjoined The Two Brewers' yard, its quiet owner always busy framing and invariably wearing a green baize apron. A lugubrious brick house next door, once fronted with trees, had anonymous inhabitants. It was wrongly associated with another Aylesbury character. Mr Holloway, pince-nezed, long-legged, trilby hatted, thin rolled umbrella, always strode past at high speed. (He was "the scissor's man" from *Struwelpeter*.) Chamberlain's garage sat beside the wide alley way at the end of which there were the remains of a smithy. The smell of hot oil announced the approach to Davies' fish and chip shop ("A great money-spinner"). The Plough and Harrow brought Buckingham Street to an end. All of these latter premises faced across the street to the back of buildings that fronted on Kingsbury. They included the formidable brick bulk that was the warehouse where Gulliver's stored beer and wine and the former slaughterhouse that was sited behind Ware's the butchers.

Buckingham Street rejoiced in a number of lime trees which gave off a strong scent when in bloom. Ponies and traps, horse-drawn delivery vans, cumbersome wagons distributing heavy goods brought by rail were drawn by dock-tailed horses and weary-looking drivers. There were occasional buses and lorries, motorcycles and side-cars and an increasing number of vehicles of varying reliability. The names of cars began to register – Bean, Riley, Ford, Sunbeam, Jowett. On Wednesdays the flow of traffic was disturbed by cattle and sheep bound for the market. They brought the sounds of the countryside to town; the smells too. The animals were viewed with suspicion by the shopkeepers, for plate-glass windows offered challenging reflections to bullocks and cows with calves. Doves cooed on roof tops and there were always fan-tailed pigeons to be seen. Aylesbury also had plenty of pigeon fanciers whose small flocks circled regularly. On late summer and early autumn nights, bats swooped as low as the lampposts. There were swifts and swallows in springtime. Some built their nests under the eves of Buckingham Street buildings.

Most of the properties in Buckingham Street were family homes and in most of them there were children. And, for the children, it seemed natural that there should be a living-in maid (not a nursemaid and she was never called a "housemaid"). Indeed, some families also employed a "daily" for general cleaning. Most of the houses had a side or back door as well as a front door. To it came the milkman, the laundry man, the delivery man, the coalman, the window-cleaner and occasional strange men called "coleporters" (another funny word for children).

The maids were mostly the daughters of the large families of farm labourers in the villages of the Vale. They were young and, as time went by, it seemed that it was the common practice to find husbands and settle in the town. The surnames of the Dollies, Edies and Marys were rarely known by children, though they might be Mrs So-and-So's Dolly or Mary. In only two houses in the street (so far as can be recalled) did the maids wear the customary black dress, white apron and white cap over the pinned-up hair. It was into this setting at Number 37 – the former Boughton property – that another William was born in July 1915.[1]

III

LIVING OVER THE SHOP

Number 37 Buckingham Street had – indeed has – a relatively narrow frontage. From its first floor bay window there are views up and down the street. On the second storey, two windows looked directly across to St Mary's Church. The rear elevation of the house was identical with that of number 39 (since pulled down) in the brickwork of which there was a stone bearing the date 1820.

Towards the end of the nineteenth century, the property was acquired by the Boughton brothers who converted it into a grocery and provision store.[2] First, they extended the buildings back towards New Street, adding a kitchen, dining-room and two bedrooms. Beyond them was a back yard a wash-house with a large copper, a warehouse as well as a stable big enough to accommodate two horses and a substantial cart. (The stable later became a garage.) Above these latter buildings were two large store rooms or lofts. Bricks on either side of the loft windows bore the initials of the Boughton brothers. Underneath the original Buckingham Street house was a long cellar. It was duplicated beneath the two adjoining houses. Originally, there had been a well at the back of the house. When the extension was built, the well was incorporated halfway down a flight of stone steps that led from the warehouse to the cellar. After the failure of the Boughton brothers business, the property was acquired by Leopold and William Mead of Stewkley. It must have been a challenging experience for two batchelors to settle in this rambling property with a view to starting afresh a business which had recently gone bankrupt.[3]

The private access to the property was in Cambridge Place. A short corridor led to a sizeable kitchen, across from which was a dining-room, remembered for a fireplace in which a fire burnt daily throughout winter. It had a black marble surround of what was reported to be Buckingham marble.[4]

Opposite to the dining-room was a staircase to the first floor. It was lit by a skylight of coloured glass which could be raised to give access to the attic. At the top of the staircase, a broad landing gave way to a corridor which led to the front of the house. On the second floor there were three bedrooms, one of which was a playroom with nursery-rhyme characters papering the walls. From the top back bedroom the entire panorama of the hills from Weedon to Aston Abbots and Ivinghoe could be seen. Two cats had the run of the domestic premises, occasionally marooning themselves on the rooftops and intermittently relieving themselves of unwanted kittens which someone had to drown. In the back yard, flying ants caused a brief panic when they swarmed.

The shop, small though it was, had been extravagantly appointed in the best Victorian style. All of the shelves were mahogany faced and there were innumerable small drawers. Could there ever have been a sufficient variety of products to fill them? Cloves, nutmegs, peppercorns, allspice, dried chillies, almonds, desiccated coconut, turmeric, curry powders were all loose and had to be weighed by the ounce. There were two glass-fronted cupboards containing oils and bottles of essences. A row of handsomely lacquered bins with lift-up lids received the contents of foil-lined, plywood tea chests and roasted coffee beans. Coffee was ground as required in a hand-turned coffee mill. Butter beans, rice, dried peas and lentils were kept in other bins.

There was a long marble shelf for cheese, butter and bacon. There were no refrigerators, but the cellar was cool even in the hottest summer. Butter pats, knives, a steel sharpener and a bacon saw were at the ready. There was also a cheese wire for cutting triangles of cheese. In front of the counter, there were rows of biscuit tins. They bore bright labels and strange names – Nice, Mane, Osbourne, Garibaldi, Bourbon. Half a dozen different kinds of paper bags (blue for white sugar, brown for brown sugar) and balls of twine and string for the endless parcels and packages were suspended near the hand-operated cash till with its long paper roll on which entries were written. On the till sat a box of either peppermint creams, crystallised ginger or chocolate ginger from which customers who settled bills knew that they could help themselves.

As Christmas approached, boxes of dried fruits multiplied – of sultanas, currants and raisins, tightly pressed, with lacy paper round the edges of the boxes and little bows of ribbon stuck into the fruit. There were boxes of sticky dates and figs, of even stickier glacé cherries and strange green lengths of crystallised angelica.

In summer, fruit was brought for sale. Cherries came in wicker-work baskets from Prestwood – red, black and "white hearts". Victoria plums, greengages and damsons attracted wasps. Pears followed summer apples. Hazelnuts, still in their green calixes, sometimes came, though minus calixes they arrived more generally in sacks at Christmas time together with walnuts and Brazil nuts. Farmers sometimes brought rabbits, hares and pheasants. Seasonally, big horse-mushrooms arrived. In spring there came occasional gifts of lamb's tails ("Lamb's tails from Shakespeare" they were called).

Disinfectants had to be kept at a discreet distance from other products. Dark red Lifebuoy soap offended with its pervasive smell; yellow Sunlight soap, a washing day favourite, was inoffensive, while furniture polish only had a remote smell. Soda was weighed by the pound in brown bags and regularly used as a cleaner. There was a mysterious object called a "blue bag" which was supposed to make washed products whiter. Starch came in packets with a robin on the cover. No respectable laundry was without it. Izal was widely used "to kill germs".

At some time there must have been a cashier in the shop, for there was a little office which had a large fixed desk with a sloping lid, holes for red and black inkwells and an upright telephone. The storeroom immediately behind the shop was furnished with equally shiny mahogany fittings, with cupboards and more small drawers. It had a cupboard in which a stock of sherry and port was kept. There was a weighing machine with a platform on which one learned to weigh oneself – and to guess the weight of others. The shop itself had a fine pair of brass scales, with pans and weights varying from half an ounce to a pound. There was also a sturdier pair to weigh heavier products up to six pounds. Someone called the Weights and Measures Man came at intervals to inspect them.

Men called commercial travellers came to collect orders for wholesalers. They were not welcomed on market days, but on other occasions they would intersperse their sales talk with travellers' tales. Sometimes, tramps ventured in. Having collected bread from the nearby baker's, they would beg for something to go with it. It was said that they made marks on the premises of those tradespeople who might be sympathetic to them.

There was much so-called "paper work". There were counter-books with carbon paper and counterfoils. The counterfoil books were kept for several years. There was headed notepaper. There were till rolls, yards of which had to be added up daily. There were ledgers, blotting paper, pens (only "Relief" nibs were accept-able) and inks (always Stephens). Once a year, a special book was bought and an apparently stressful exercise took place in it. It was called stock-taking and it called for several days of early rising.

Stock taking was important. It was believed that the Boughton brothers went bankrupt because they were insufficiently alert to the need. Possibly, too, they over-invested in 37 Buckingham Street, the appointments of which must have been superior to those of their Bicester Road home – right down to the Carrara marble fireplace in the drawing-room (beneath the shelf of which W.R.B. had inscribed his initials).

The so-called drawing-room had an upright piano with a stool crammed with sheet music (the legacy of a musical mother). There are distinct memories of two other features. One was a French ormolu clock surmounted by a boy with a fishing rod. It had ceased to function and was covered by an intriguing glass dome. The other was a wind-up phonograph with an accompany-ing red-lined box which contained the residue of a dozen or more fragile cylindrical wax records. Against the background of a crackly tune and preceded by the spoken words "This is an His Master's Voice recording" two tunes were played. One was a laughing song with continuous variations on the theme "Ha-ha". Only the refrain of the other is remembered. "And they didn't get far upon the journey, Oh no, Oh no."

As with every dwelling, the house had its problems. Every window was operated with sash cords. The cords rotted intermittently; the window frames swelled intermittently. It was a struggle to open and close them: they squeaked and groaned in the process. But they had to be opened, because it was healthier that way. Certainly, bedroom windows must be kept ajar all night. Naturally, all of the rooms had fireplaces. The wind made organ-like noises down the chimneys. Fires were rarely lit in the bedrooms unless anyone was ill. There was always the fear that a chimney would catch fire and the sweep came at the drop of a hat if soot fell into a fireplace. Coal had to be carried up from one of the warehouses. There was no running water in any of the bedrooms and the bathroom was primitive. Hot water had to be delivered in large enamel jugs from the kitchen to the basins on the marble-topped washstands. In cold winter weather, when frost flowers decorated the window panes, there was constant fear about frozen pipes. Water was known to freeze in the jug on the washstand.

Earliest recollections of the house are of limited gaslight, with gas mantles dissolving in a minor snow shower at the touch of a finger or even the brush of a moth's wing. There was no gas in the bedrooms, so that there was a large number of candlesticks, with candles of various sizes, the wax of which formed fanciful shapes as it dribbled in a draughty room. Matches always seemed to part company with candlesticks. The curling blue smoke and smell of an extinguished candle are more distinct memories. So, too, are the nightlights that usually flickered out before dawn broke in winter. Seemingly miles of pipes were eventually installed to enclose the electrical wiring. Everyone then became a master of light and darkness at the click of a switch. Brass switches not infrequently transmitted slight shocks and a faint "ping" announced that yet another bulb had blown itself out.

Shop and house yielded all sorts of smells. Best of all were those from the coffee mill, the tea bin and the drawers containing cloves and peppercorns. Large cheeses, gently mouldering in their dusty grey-green cheesecloths, greeted the descent into the cellar. The odour of the occasional Italian gorgonzola was the most powerful of all. The sides of Danish bacon, wrapped in sacking, and the hams, suspended on hooks until their turn came for boiling, gave off a faint smoky smell. A sour smell hung about the can beneath the vinegar barrel. In the kitchen pantry, home-made wine was brewed seasonally in large earthenware containers – elderflower, cowslip, dandelion, rhubarb, elderberry, damson, orange. Yeast, on floating islands of toasted bread, rotated gently on the surface of the wine with the process of fermentation. In the dining-room, there were the residual smells of beer, port wine, sherry and whiskey in the empty glasses left by customers who had paid their bills by cheque. They were usually farmers settling substantial accounts. Sometimes their accounts ran for six months, even a year, in the loose-leaf pigskin covered ledger.

As the days lengthened and something called "Summer time" caused clocks to be altered, sympathy was expressed to the country customers who were universal in their detestation of it. Summer implied going to bed by daylight – a dispiriting experience, because all of the daytime noises continued unabated. Moreover with all of the windows open, conversation and laughter from the dining-room next door as well as from that below floated up disturbingly. Moths began to flap around, bluebottles to buzz, the occasional mosquito to whine. Long-legged spiders and, later in the summer, daddy-long-legs found their way in from the ivy-clad wall outside. The late spring dawn chorus subsided, but one woke early just the same. It always seemed hours before it was time to get up.

IV

THE HOUSE NEXT DOOR

Next door there was an older elongated building, beamed and tile-roofed on to which the 1820 Buckingham Street building must have been grafted. Entrance was gained through an echoing passage with a loudly ticking grandfather clock. It led to a long dark dining-room, ivy-coloured within; ivy-covered walls without. A large kitchen and scullery lay beyond. The dining-room was furnished with mahogany and much highly polished silver. On the walls hung half life-sized photographs of the family.

Outside an area paved with cobblestones was bordered by a fern-covered rockery constructed of flint stones. The rockery contained a lime tree which, though frequently trimmed, sprouted with vigour, the scent of its blossoms and seasonally sticky leaves attracted many insects. Beyond grew a large red hawthorn and a thin yew. The long garden, stretching to New Street, had originally been planned with some care. A lawn gave way to a raised flower bed, faced with yet more flints and backed by a wall of upturned railway sleepers. The wall supported three classical busts – the Roman emperors as we called them. Along the east side were the cottages of Cambridge Place. They were concealed by a high wall from behind which came the sounds of their outside lavatories (one between two houses). Their laundry had to be hung on the front of the houses in Cambridge Place. Small bedroom windows prevented too much prying through an overgrown privet hedge.

Behind the Roman emperors was an asparagus bed (white with salt at certain times of the year). Then the garden dropped to a lower level, with a retaining brick wall and a row of spear-headed railings. In addition to the apple trees, there was a flourishing senna pod tree round which lilies-of-the-valley grew thickly. A fig tree thrived despite its cramped location. To the west, rising almost to the height of the Wesleyan chapel, was a splendid beech tree. The trees attracted a multitude of birds. They included ring doves, the incessant cooing of which was not fully appreciated. Owls, both hooting and screeching, came regularly. To drive them away, a pair of wooden clappers was acquired, such as bird-scarers used to frighten off pigeons. They were employed in the depth of the night from one of the bedroom windows of the house next door. A sufficient clatter was made to arouse the entire neighbourhood but not to frighten the offending owls.

The spearhead of one of the broken railings provides a childhood memory. The Roman busts indicated the possibility of Roman remains, of which we had seen something in the museum. An idle day in the summer holidays was spent excavating in the garden for likely treasure trove. Nothing materialised during the morning dig save for some inconsequential oyster shells (there were many others in our own New Street garden). However, during the lunchtime, absence of the principal digger enabled a broken spearhead from the railings to be concealed at the bottom of the excavation. It was rapidly discovered by our companion when he returned to the dig. We immediately pronounced it to be a Roman relic and he was persuaded to take it to the museum. Appropriately wrapped, it was deposited on the museum steps, the bell was rung and the discoverer retreated. The following week, a short paragraph appeared in *The Bucks Herald* inviting the anonymous discoverer to report to the curator. He was congratulated on his find and the spearhead was dispatched to the British Museum for identification. In due course, it was returned as the head of a Napoleonic cavalry lance. Subsequently it was placed in a glass case with a descriptive card and the donor's name. Perhaps, in retrospect, the identification was near enough correct. The railings might well have been disused cavalry lances from the Napoleonic period. The entire row of spearheaded railings was identical. They all had wooden cores encased in metal.

The house next door was a source of great interest in Ascot week, when the Cubitt car awaited to receive its quota of top-hatted men and appropriately dressed ladies with umbrellas and sunshades as required. Edith, the capped-and-aproned maid, might watch furtively from an upstairs window. Rory the otherwise kennelled dog, was allowed to watch the departure. Normally, his main purpose seemed to be to keep at bay the legion of cats that trespassed into the garden – and to lead the chorus of night-time barking.

V

ROUND THE TOWN

Aylesbury people went *round* the town. From a distance, St Mary's church seemed to be the central point. On the ground, it was the market place. From our nursery window, the church dominated the skyline. Near at hand, the structure that supported the clock seemed to be perched awkwardly on top of the rest of the building. The central bell tower and impressive nave deserved something better. The clock itself was much appreciated. Its accuracy was guaranteed by the assiduous Mr Marshall of Silver Street, who was also the most eminent member of the St John Ambulance Brigade.

The church was surrounded by a graveyard of considerable size with a scatter of headstones more typical of a country churchyard. Beyond, an assemblage of old cottages formed St Mary's Square. They were without front gardens and opened directly on to the pavement. When the front rooms were lit in winter, children could stare through the windows.

The main entrance to the church on the south side was not normally approached by vehicles. For weddings, which always attracted a miscellaneous crowd of onlookers, generously accompanied by prams and pushchairs, a red carpet would normally be laid down to Church Street.

In the north transept of the church (past all the bell ropes), Lady Lee's tomb intrigued children. The kneeling alabaster figures of Lady Lee and her daughter had gaunt faces. It was also pointed out that they were dressed in clothes that belonged to the reign of Queen Mary, not Queen Elizabeth – suggesting that the ladies belonged to the Catholic faith. Two little alabaster bundles on the tomb were of the children who died in infancy. It was also pointed out that, throughout history, the tomb had never been without a little red flower.

Inside the church, the fixed pews no longer commanded rents (which at one time guaranteed private occupancy) but parishioners who arrived to find their accustomed places occupied by strangers did not exactly display looks of Christian charity.

Fig. 5. Parson's Fee was an Aylesbury place name that appealed to children – the same as "Upper Hundreds" and "Turn Furlong". (Courtesy of the Aylesbury Society).

Parson's Fee, with its pointed gables and overhanging eaves, presented a traditional Christmas card scene under snow. It was one of the pleasant cottagey precincts that surrounded the church. At its far end was medieval St Osyth's house, a dwelling of interest to children because of its reputed ghost. It stood beside the high gates that shut off the four-square Prebendal House. The name of John Wilkes was associated with this residence at an early age,

Fig. 6. St Osyth's. Children could look down over the railings into the ground floor of the house. (Courtesy of the Aylesbury Society)

though not for the reason of his radical politics. ("He married a Mead", it was imparted).[5]

From the Market Square, the church was approached by way of Temple Street and Temple Square, where five streets met in a sort of star. In a stuccoed house on the south side, dwelt the appropriately named Miss Starbuck, a bright little blackbird of a woman, with a smile and a word for everybody. Temple Square contained yet another butcher's shop – though a pork butcher's this time – as well as a beautifully bay-windowed cobbler's shop,

Fig. 7. Church Street

entered up a flight of steps. The somewhat dingy offices of the Conservative Party occupied a part of another house. During election campaigns, both political parties recruited schoolchildren to trail in procession round the town, beating tin cans and containers in unison and singing, "Vote, vote, vote for Mr So-and-so" before continuing with three uncomplimentary lines about the opposing candidate. One election is remembered because there was a Conservative victory and fireworks were exploded in the head-quarters' garden which backed on to Temple School playground. Diplomatic relations between educationalists and politicians were temporarily strained.

From Temple Square, the church was approached by way of Church Street, architecturally the most distinguished street in Aylesbury. Dr Parrott's plate identified the occupant of the first, plain-faced brick house. Kindly Dr Coventon (his winter overcoat always seemed too big for him) and his Councillor wife (nutria furred in hat as well as in coat) lived in the intriguing Chantry House, with its diamond-shaped, leaded window panes. Opposite rose the classical façade of Ceeley House with its garden and coach house behind double gates. It was the home of Dr Baker (who was reputed to have brought me into the world). After his death, his popular daughter Cicely lived there for a number of years. Next door was the museum, formerly the old Grammar School. It struck children as a rather dull and musty place. There were tall glass cases in what had probably been the principal schoolroom. They were filled with beady-eyed birds and beasts identified with yellowing labels. There were displays of archaeological remains and some fragments of Roman glass and earthenware which made a mark. Little flint arrowheads were described as "elves' arrows", but best of all was the penny farthing bicycle included among the Aylesbury memorabilia.

Across the street was the home of Miss Hunt, a Jenny wren to Miss Starbuck's blackbird. Her house was also headquarters of something called the Zenana Mission, but on Sunday afternoons at 2.30 p.m. it became a private Sunday School attended by about twenty children. Beyond a low, dark entrance hall there was a heavily curtained dining-room with a harmonium. Upstairs there was a panelled drawing-room with a piano. Miss Hunt played mission hymns on each with great gusto. On one table there was a porcelain bowl filled with never-to-be-forgotten clove balls which were surreptitiously sniffed. They probably came from the Zanzibar branch of the Zenana mission.

To the north of the church, beyond the high railings of the somewhat neglected churchyard, was a quiet residential area where the streets had rather grand-sounding names —Granville, Ripon. Whitehall. A Masonic Lodge sat incongruously among the terraced houses of Ripon Street. ("What is a Masonic Lodge?")

Church Street backed on to Castle Street ("Where is the castle?"). Castle Street was popular with children because of its elevated pavements protected by iron railings. Through low, lace-curtained windows, it was possible to peep into the ground-floor rooms of some of the old houses. Here, too, lived and operated another coal merchant, Mr East. On the corner of Parson's Fee and Castle Street, with a walled garden, was St Mary's vicarage. It was associated with the names of a succession of canons – Whitechurch (it was said that he was a novelist), Pepys, Howard. Down a steep slope, flanked by cottages (at seven to ten shillings a week rent)

Fig. 8. Green End House, Rickford's Hill

was Oxford Road. To the right was The Hen and Chickens. To the left the road led to Rickford's Hill.

At the top of Rickford's Hill, there was a row of dark red brick houses with intriguing garret windows. Side by side were the Friends' Meeting House and *The Saracen's Head*. ("What was a Saracen and what happened to his head?") Rickford's Hill was also graced by Green End House, the most handsome house in Aylesbury. In summer, special journeys were made to look at the ropes of wisteria, with their pale lilac flowers, that hung in bunches beside the cream stucco walls.

In turn, Rickford's Hill led to Bourbon Street. The name, so far as children were concerned, stood for biscuits rather than the French royal family. It was an exciting street for two reasons. First, it accommodated the fire station. The horse-drawn machine was still to be seen, though it had long been replaced by a highly polished motor vehicle. There was also another vehicle with an extension ladder. The fire brigade was captained by the owner of the town's best shoe shop. He was assisted among others by the curate from St Mary's church. When they put in an appearance on official occasions, their brass helmets were much admired.

The second reason why Bourbon Street has left its mark is because of Aylesbury swimming baths. Outside the rather gloomy entrance there was also a notice advertising "slipper baths". No one knew what a slipper bath was, who used it or, indeed, where it was in the building. In the swimming baths, the water was changed at the weekend. It was very cold on Mondays. On Fridays, the water was unhealthily soupy, the tiled bottom dangerously slippery, the atmosphere heavy and steamy. Facilities for changing and other purposes were primitive. Needless to say, there was no mixed bathing. One day was reserved for ladies. The admission charge fell towards the end of the week. Not surprisingly, few Aylesburians were able to swim.

Across the road from the entrance to the baths was Friarage House, its windows and doors inviting any vehicle which took the corner too quickly. At its corner was Friarage Passage which ran parallel with Great Western Street. It was a long cobbled footpath between the high walls of invisible gardens. It led down to a little railed bridge which spanned the reedy Bear Brook. Here, seasonally, tadpoles and sticklebacks were netted and put into jam jars by small boys. In Friarage Passage, there was also a plain faced building behind a tall iron-barred fence. It bore the name The Comrades Club. (Questions were asked, of course. "What is a Friarage?" "Who are the comrades?")

The town yielded plenty of cooking smells – commercial and domestic. Those from half a dozen bakers were complemented by those of boiled cabbage or of saucepans boiling over – for many kitchen doors opened on to the street. Bourbon Street was noted for its roasting coffee beans: Buckingham Street, for its fish and chips. Competing with the latter was the intermittently distinctive smell from the blacksmith as he tried a red hot shoe on a horse's hoof. Laundry smells were not uncommon in the central parts of the town. Seasonally, there were tarry smells associated with road surfacing and of trees, such as the lime tree, in bloom.

More subtle were the scents from ladies as they passed – the readily recognised odour of eau-de-Cologne and lavender water. Early in winter came the faint smell of mothballs from fur coats which had attempted to elude the assault of summer moths. And there were the distinctive smells of fabrics sold in shops, tweedy, cottony, woolly smells. (A neighbour's daughter, commenting on dress material, actually declared, "It smells good quality").

Since pipes and cigarettes were smoked ubiquitously (the former a definite sign of masculinity), varieties of tobacco could be named from passing smoke. Cigar smoke was reserved for indoors. The smell of beer – usually stale beer – was evident as the open door of one of the town's many public houses was passed.

VI

THE MARKET SQUARE

All roads led to the Market Square. Its focus was the clock tower that, for some reason, always looked older than its years. The Square was presided over by John Hampden, his fine statue the icon of Aylesbury. Discretely to his left and appropriately beside a bank, the more recent figure of Benjamin Disraeli stood in his robes. At the top of the Square beside the simple, clean–cut war memorial, the clearest memories are of two shops. Flanking the cobbled passage to The King's Head were John Field's fine old

Fig. 9. The Market Square from the Town Hall arches – its rather gloomy double-doored entrance to the right. Above was a mayor function room – a long climb up a flight of stairs. (Nick Parker's sketch omits the lions!) (Courtesy of the Aylesbury Society). The two Market Square icons – John Hampden and Benjamin Disraeli – are added.

silversmiths, its windows covered with steel grills and G. M. Adam's cosy old sweet-smelling tobacconists. With its fine mullioned window and courtyard (in the lofts above what had formerly been the stables, we used to play) The King's Head seemed to lack the status that it deserved. It was the oldest of the inns on the Market Square, but The Bull's Head took pride of place. It was inseparable from its owner, the jovial, rubicund Giacomo Gargini, a popular townsman who looked his best in his mayoral robes. The Bull's Head had a mock-Tudor façade with leaded windows which probably concealed a late eighteenth-century interior on to which had been grafted a ballroom. Strictly speaking it was the only ballroom in town, others which employed that title being merely dance halls. From the Market Square to the High Street, there was an alleyway called Hale Leys. On the north-east side of the Square, there were three banks, all sufficiently impressive with their high ceilings, mahogany counters and brass weighing machines. There were little copper shovels for scooping up the coins from the polished counter. Copper coins went into blue bags; silver coins into buff-coloured bags. Children collected "Bun pennies" – pennies which had been minted when Queen Victoria's head on the coin showed her hair with a "bun". Mr Hall, the Bank Manager, always wore a dark blue suit with a starched white collar and tie.

The south side of the Square had the commanding presence of the baroque County Court House, architecturally unappreciated by the young. Curiosity was aroused principally by the ground-level windows with bars over them which were reputed to be the cells in which miscreants were kept who were awaiting trial. Opposite the Court House an indestructible pair of lions peacefully crouched on either side of the military statue of Lord Chesham. The Bell Hotel, on the corner of Walton Street, seemed to turn its back on the older White Swan. Across from it, there were Boait's rather steamy tearooms and Jones and Cox's hardware store, best remembered for the gardening implements, the autumn bulbs and spring seed potatoes that overflowed on to the pavement.

Half of the Market Square had sturdy iron railings to which cattle had probably been tied in former times, but which now served the young as bars on which to turn somersaults. On Wednesdays and more particularly Saturdays, the Square was alive with the open air market. Some stalls are recalled; others, forgotten. The china and glass stall (seconds presumably) is remembered for the way in which the storeholder, more auctioneer than storeholder, built up precariously balanced tea services and other wares as he asked for bids from likely customers. The sweet and confectionery merchant auctioned similar piles of boxes of cheap chocolates and sweets (no one seemed to ask where they had come from). There was Sid and Sam's second-hand clothing stall. There were highly competitive fruit and vegetable stalls and springtime plant stalls, all under flapping canvas. The Salvation Army instrumentalists and singers took up their positions (often by John Hampden). They usually mustered about a score. Two local characters regularly passed by. Both were small, shuffling and had ornithological nicknames – "Pigeon" Green and "Peewit", who had no known surname.

The Town Hall was grafted, with no architectural concessions, on to the County Court House. Its big archway led by way of Loader's corn and hay business, to the new cattle market and the uninspiring recreation ground. Sometimes, the Town Hall was called the Corn Exchange. It served many purposes. Several times a week it became a cinema. Rows of wooden chairs provided uncomfortable seating on the ground floor, with three more rows in the balcony. Tickets were torn off rolls suspended above the cashier in the pay box – 6d., 9d. and 1/3 upstairs. Lantern slides advertising businesses in the town preceded the black and white silent films – always the same slides. There was rarely a full house, there was a lot of noisy scuffling among the cheaper seats. All in all, it was rather a bleak place.

Once a year, however, the Town Hall exuded warmth when it accommodated Albert Smith's benefit for the Royal Bucks Hospital. All and sundry came to fill the dance floor, to play "progressive" whist upstairs (tea and coffee only), to patronise the downstairs bar and to await the immense prize draw. Gifts were extracted from all the tradespeople – boxes of candied fruits, tins of biscuits, bottles of wines and spirits, sacks of coal. On other

Fig. 10. The King's Head.

occasions, the Town Hall was the setting for something called The
Mayor's Reception (black ties and evening dresses). The wooden
chairs were fetched out again for the audiences that attended the
annual performances of the local Gilbert and Sullivan opera
group.[6] A temporary stage was erected, curtains were suspended to

billow in the draughts, scenery and costumes were hired (costumes usually of uncertain fit). There was an active prompter and an orchestra which obviously longed for its moments of crescendo. The crescendos also helped to drown out the uncertain pitch of some of the soloists. The perennial leading performers appeared to allocate to themselves the leading roles for the next season before the final curtain was drawn. "Next season, we hope..."

For children, the most intriguing part of the Market Square was the little warren of alleyways that focused on The Dark Lantern. Here, interminable games of hide-and-seek and chase-me could be played. There were three entrances from Silver Street and three from the Market Square. Silver Street was dominated by the backs of the Market Square houses, probably Georgian in age, as was most of Silver Street itself. The only recollections of Silver Street are of the clockmakers at the entrance, Hewitt's pork butcher's shop and Solloway's grocery at the opposite end.

Two of the passages led into Market Street and ran alongside the inviting chinaware shop, stocking all the best of Staffordshire ware, of the small Miss Dukes's. They looked rather like porcelain figures themselves – there was something Toby-jug-like about

Fig. 11. The King's Head.

them. On the other side of Market Street was Wood's the florists, which never seemed to have much for sale, but everything was of the highest quality. There were choice greenhouse fruits from the nurseries of Waddesdon Manor. The smell of freshly picked carnations still lingers in the memory. Next door was Smith's, the foremost of the town's butchers. Its proprietors were straw-hatted, white-aproned, red-faced and shiny-booted. They had a gleaming range of cleavers, saws and knives and a great wooden chopping block upon a generously sawdusted floor. Their Christmas fat stock display was a sight never to be forgotten. A wooden frame was erected outside the shop. It groaned with overweight beef carcasses (beribboned with prize certificates), half pigs, turkeys, pheasants and other poultry. The entrance to the house over the shop was in the back alleyway opposite The King's Head. Upstairs there lived the alert ninety-year old Granny Smith. She extended a hand one day. "Hold this," she said, "then you can say that you have held the hand of someone who was taken to witness the last public hanging in Aylesbury." (Public hanging was abolished in 1868).

The Market Square was the setting for annual events which attracted the entire town. It was the scene for the regular visits of travelling fairs. Mrs Pettigrew's roundabouts (merry-go-rounds, perhaps: carousels, never) were most popular. No other round-abouts could compare with her galloping horses. The horses had particularly fierce eyes and blood-red nostrils. As they went round in groups of three, the outermost were the best because they went fastest.[7] The edges to which the striped canvas roof was attached bore scenes from Alma, Balaclava, Inkerman and Sebastopol. There was much polished brass and there were many electric light bulbs. Perforated paper turned slowly behind the gilded steam organ to emit martial tunes with wooden Nubian maidens tapping tambourines in time. A giant highly-polished steam engine generated power in front of Lord Cheshams's statue. A nearby cakewalk was a lesser attraction, with its own diminutive organ. The swings, which sat uncertainly upon the cobblestones, had long bell-pull ropes. There were coconut shies and other sideshows which had their garish collections of prizes – brightly dressed dolls, cheap coloured glassware and chinaware. There was a small roundabout for children which was turned by a muscular man. From all of these amusements, grubby men collected masses of silver and copper coins and delivered them to a crimson-painted caravan with cut-glass windows. Inside, like a spider in a web, sat a lady in black satin with jet beads. Before her, the coins were piled high upon the table. It was Mrs Pettigrew herself (at least so it was said).

There was one stall which attracted everybody by its smell. The peppermint rock, toffee apples and brittle nut toffee were irresistible. The toffee mixture was tossed up over a hook, pulled at like a skein of wool, worked with floury hands and finally flopped down on a slab of marble upon which it was cut into lengths and squares. ("Don't touch it. It is made from damaged sugar – and they don't wash their hands," were the parental warnings.) Pink and white coconut ice were also sold. By night each sideshow had its own lamps and lanterns, with the smell of naphtha and paraffin mingling with that of hot oil and steam. Sideshows included The Seal Man found swimming in Arctic waters, with flippers instead of arms, the giant rats (musquashes?) and the Spider Woman – a head with spider's legs and body, the rest of the dark-eyed lady disappearing by some trick with mirrors.

Sometimes, the less appealing Thurston's fair appeared. No galloping horses here, but a staid circle of gilded and carved gondolas. Each gondola was presided over by some classical or mythical creature. Seated upon dusty velvet-padded seats, there rose up in front of one a Greek god or a Triton, a Merman or a dragon. All were somewhat the worse for wear and they vibrated unsteadily on threepenny rides which ended all too quickly. Occasionally, life-sized posters in bright colours would announce that a circus was coming to town. A great tent would appear in a muddy meadow off Cambridge Street (the inadequate site resulted in an eventual move to the first meadow in Buckingham Road). There are clear memories of elephants on parade and, in particular, three passing up Buckingham Street, trunks to tail, on their way to advertise their circus to a crowd of admirers in the Market Square.

Also to the Market Square, as they had done for many years, came the Whaddon Chase Foxhounds on their annual meet. Scores of horses and riders would arrive from all round the Vale (it was, of course, before the days of horse boxes and lorries). Clipped and pampered hunters would mingle with shaggy ponies. Grooms waited with pairs of horses and ponies on leading reins for their owners to arrive in chauffeur-driven cars. Respectable ladies were expected to ride side-saddle. For women to ride astride was still not quite acceptable. Top hats and bowler hats (tinplated in the crown) dominated. For men, they were clipped with a retaining string to their jackets. Most women wore a veil over their half top hats or bowlers. Black hunting caps were very much in the minority. For ladies, black habits took precedence over grey or fawn – the latter being considered somewhat theatrical. Ladies might wear Parma violets in their buttonholes. Men were denied this touch. Restless horses slipped and slithered all too easily on the granite setts. A red bow on a hunter's tail was a sign that it might kick. The inns on the Square doubled their trade for an hour or so before the cavalcade moved off, though hospitality in the form of a stirrup cup was usually expected by the riders. No one pondered the consequences of alcohol on the hunting field – indeed, it was supposed to stimulate the sport. A hip flask was not infrequently carried to supplement the intake. Departure was usually down Buckingham Road or Bicester Road by way of Buckingham Street – that is to say in the direction of the Whaddon Chase country (for the territoriality of individual hunts was something that was jealously guarded). It was regularly rumoured that the Prince of Wales would join the hunt, but Aylesbury never saw him, though he was reputedly seen at Whitchurch, Cubblington, Dunton and Waddesdon. Sometimes, later in the day, invariably mudbespattered, hunters would return through the town.

Cows and bullocks, no less than horses, slipped and skidded on the granite setts as they passed through the Square on market days. Wednesday was the principal market day, though there were some sales on Saturdays. Cattle would be driven to town by professional drovers who would do their best to keep individual herds apart from each other. The Vale of Aylesbury had a network of market towns, all within about ten or twelve miles of each other. Flocks of sheep moved more speedily, but generally with less control. From the market pens, they moved into the auction hall which was loud with the gabble of the auctioneer, the high priest of the market. The return from the market was frequently more chaotic than the arrival. Frightened animals might bolt down side streets – even into shops. A High Street mêlée of two different flocks of sheep is recalled. They piled into the National Provincial Bank and could not find their way out. They climbed two steps into Janes's the fishmongers. Not long afterwards, a cow with a calf caught sight of herself in a plate glass window – and Jarvis's millinery display was badly deranged.

The offending granite setts, gift of a local benefactor, were eventually moved from much of the centre of the town and replaced by wooden blocks from Australia ("The same as in Oxford Street"). It was rapidly discovered that in wet weather they presented a different kind of slippery surface. They, too, had to be removed. The setts found their way into a number of private gardens around the town. The wooden blocks, tar-impregnated, found their way into many an open fireplace. They were probably the cause of a fair number of chimney fires.

Fire brought an unhappy change to the Market Square. It destroyed the Market Theatre. The theatre stood a little way up a narrow passage beside *The Green Man Inn* (the name intrigued children but was never explained to them.) The theatre was a cosy, galleried building from before the First World War. It was the home of travelling repertory companies, of variety acts and of an annual pantomime. By the time that the first version of *Ben Hur* was circulating, the theatre had been rebuilt. A great fuss was made about the film. There were life-sized portraits of the actors in the passage way. An "augmented orchestra" was also advertised. It was disappointing to find that these words meant no more than that to the customary piano were added a trumpet, drums and a violin. All the episodes covering the chariot race were accompanied by the overture to *The Marriage of Figaro* (which remained the incidental music to *Ben Hur* for many years).

Fig. 12. Silver Street.

The Market Square witnessed other annual events. Armistice Day was celebrated on the eleventh day of the eleventh month. It mattered not on which day the eleventh fell, all of the rituals were carried out regardless of any inconvenience that might be caused. A full blown ceremony was held – the corps of veterans, medals tinkling, bowler hats mingling with cloth caps, were preceded by a band and followed by the Territorial Army, the St John Ambulance and other organisations. Everyone wore Flanders poppies – some of expensive silk; some of cheap fabric. The Two Minutes' Silence was rigidly observed. In schools there was an extra assembly and two minutes seemed an awfully long time. Everything came to a standstill – even hospitals, it was said. On the eleventh hour all of the factory hooters in the town were sounded, beginning with the stentorian Rivet Works' hooter ("What were bifurcated rivets?" we asked). Stationary railway engines blew their whistles. Hats were removed from male heads. At the war memorial the Last Post was sounded. Poppy wreaths were laid. Hail, rain or shine, the band struck up. "O God our help in ages past" was already a hymn sacred to the day. It seemed out of place on any other.

Bereavements from the war years were still common, especially as a result of the aftermath of mustard gas. There were also signs of war wounds – wooden legs, crutches, false arms, hands short of fingers, patched eyes. The shadow of the Spanish 'flu also remained. It was with strange feelings that one went to the cemetery with its odd Gothic chapels, to visit the marble angels that were family memorials to its toll. The slow movement of funeral processions through the streets of the town is recalled. St Mary's church bell often tolled on these occasions. Horse-drawn hearses and coaches had not yet been entirely replaced by motor vehicles. Hats had to be lifted as they passed by. Mourning outfits were advertised by local milliners. "Widow's weeds" were still to be seen. Not to take to black clothes was a sign of disrespect. Men might retain black ties, black armbands or black diamonds on their sleeves for several weeks. Black-edged envelopes and notepaper were used for correspondence.

Two other events enlivened the Market Square: a special

procession when the Assize Court went into session; and Mayor's
Sunday. The Assize Judge in wig and robes proceeded from his
lodgings behind the Court House with his entourage. The High
Sheriff, the wigged town clerk, the mayor, magistrates, other
officials and local dignitaries, preceded by the top-hatted mace
bearer – umbrellas up if it rained – walked up Temple Street and
Church Street to be met at the church entrance by the vicar. A
special service was then held before the return to deal with the
Court's business.

Temple Street could hardly have been of interest to the judicial
company, but it is remembered personally because of the music
shop where the first uninspiring exercise books were bought,
because of Izzard's picture-framing shop (the name enabled us to
christen it either Gizzard or Lizard) and because of the Literary
Institute. It was disappointing to discover that there was little
literature inside the Institute, rather the click of billiard balls and
the faint smell of alcohol.

On Mayor's Sunday, preceded by a band and the mace-bearer,
came the mayor and mayoress. The mayor was red-robed,
musquash-furred and cock-hatted. He was followed by a procession
of town councillors. Territorial Army recruits, the police, St John
Ambulance volunteers, scouts, guides, even wolf cubs. Few
members in the procession other than the territorials attempted to
keep in step with the band. Most looked somewhat embarrassed
and sheepish as they shuffled through the thin crowd of onlookers
who lined the pavements. ("Here comes so-and-so" was usually
followed by some unflattering comment.) It often seemed to rain.
Then the dignitaries became a column of bobbing black umbrellas
and the uniformed followers looked more and more dejected and
damp.

Kingsbury, a triangular appendage to the Market Square, seemed
to miss all of the fun. At its centre there was a rather unpleasant
object – a tank from the First World War. Its caterpillar tracks
were very rusted. No one appeared to know how it arrived there.
It was a happy day when it was removed. Kingsbury had three
public houses, The Red Lion leaving the strongest impression
because it had a model red lion over the entrance. The biggest

Fig. 13. Kingsbury. The fountain was eventually removed to the Vale. The tank exploded when it was being dismantled.

building in Kingsbury bore the title The Victoria Working Men's Club. Next-door-but-one was Aylesbury's leading electrical firm – Mackrill's. Kingsbury contained Holden's, the town's best tailors and breeches makers, its prices always in guineas instead of pounds. Samuel's Printing Office was the source of the literature produced for Edgar Wallace's unsuccessful candidature as a Liberal parliamentarian for the mid-Bucks constituency. His smooth profile, with a cigarette in a long holder is still recalled. The handsome Georgian house of the Shaw family (Jean another teacher of pianoforte) had a grand piano in a room with French windows opening on to a walled garden. Otherwise, Kingsbury conjures up memories of an olfactory nature. There are those of leather from Ivatts, the best shoe shop in town, of vinegar and beer from empty barrels in Gulliver's warehouse, and of the various seeds and petfoods from Wheeler's seed shop. The mingled odours of scented soaps and disinfectants emanated from Jane's the chemists. Here, great glass flasks of green and red fluid – signs of the trade, gleamed in the windows above a congested miscellany of pharmaceutical products. This was the source of cod liver oil and eucalyptus, camphorated oil and lung tonic, as well as other remedies for winter's ills.

There was a contrasting gloom in Jowett's (sometime, Bradford's), the ironmongers next door. It was unique in Aylesbury – a minor emporium filled with countless tools, pots and pans, fire irons, locks, catches and shelves of boxes containing every type of screw, nail and hook imaginable. It was an Aladdin's cave for the 1920s handyman. There was a lurking oily smell in summer and in winter a strong smell of paraffin. In keeping with the trade, there was a man in brown overalls who dealt in a ponderous and deliberate manner with customers – quite different from the brisk, white-coated pharmacist next door.

At the opposite corner of the Market Square from Kingsbury was Great Western Street. Another butcher and baker as well as another abandoned slaughterhouse were round the comer that was occupied by yet another public house. Beyond, up a flight of steps, stood a prim house with white net curtains which accommodated someone called The Registrar of Births, Marriages and Deaths. The prim but pleasant Foster family "lived above the shop". On the same side, beyond some run-down property, were the extensive stables and hay lofts of the Seaton family. The lofts were a fine playground in wet weather. Opposite stood the Railway Inn, red brick with stained-glass windows, a seemingly lifeless place, but enlivened for children by its elaborate ridge tiling which sprouted terracotta dragons.

Great Western Street led to an unpretentious little station, with shunting yards and sheds to meet the needs of the engines. Rows of unlocked carriages sat in the railway sidings. They were furnished with ancient stuffed seats, leather-strapped windows, uncertain heating facilities and outdated sepia photographs. There was the occasional non-smoking compartment as well as one or two compartments per train marked LADIES ONLY. There were no toilet facilities. But the station was more than the terminus for a branch of the Great Western system and the northern end of the Metropolitan Railway. It was on the Great Central route, receiving expresses which stopped on their way from Marylebone to Manchester. Always assuming the attractions of the wickerwork-and-palm-tree tea lounge at Marylebone station were resisted, it was possible to enjoy a tea for one shilling and threepence on the hour-long journey to Aylesbury before the train proceeded to all sorts of improbably named stations northwards.

On the other side of the railway tracks lay California. It was approached by a sturdy wooden footbridge on which it was considered exciting to stand in the smoke and steam that rose from passing trains. Beyond, there were cinder trackways, edged in spring with coltsfoot, a sprinkling of houses that had a lost look in the midst of overgrown bushes, several garden plots and the Bear Brook ("How did it get its name?" we always asked). There was also a rather dismal workshop advertising itself as an ink works. No place in Aylesbury seemed less appropriately named than California.

California lay at the approaches to Aylesbury race course. A footpath through two fields led to an open stretch of country which, once a year, was the site of a meeting. In retrospect, it always seemed to be March when the meetings were held. East winds blew and there was mud under foot. Rough stands were erected for spectators; carrier's carts and wagonettes providing alternative accommodation. Boots, socks and trousers suffered because the gumboot was rarely worn. Bookies gabbled their odds on soap box stands under big umbrellas. Their clerks stood beneath them with heavy leather bags slung round their necks or over their shoulders. Women were few and far between.

VII

WALTON STREET AND HIGH STREET

While roads seemed to trail off into the country, streets were a central feature of the town. Both Walton Street and High Street commanded the Market Square in their different ways.

Walton Street had the curiosity of a pawnbroker's shop – Lucas's. The three balls were prominently displayed. In one window, there was a sparkling display of jewellery, each item with a clearly priced ticket on which the item was also described. In another window, there was a display of second-hand goods and cheap clothes. Next door stood a fine double-fronted house with a broad bay window which bore the name Lepper (for children, a name which immediately recalled biblical stories). In fact, the brass plate announced a veterinary surgeon. The white, stuccoed, bow-windowed Viney house was a little farther down the hill. It was one of the two most attractive houses in the whole town. Next to its walled garden over which lime trees peeped, stood the Stopford residence. It remained that long after the Lord Stopford became the Earl of Courtown. Few, if any, would have recognised it by its official name, The Old House. The long, stuccoed, porched

Fig. 14. The Hazell House on Walton Road was destroyed by bombs in 1940.

Fig. 15. The Old House, more commonly known as the Stopford and (later) the Courtown House, had an extensive almost park like area behind the formidable Walton Street front. (see OS Map, Figure 2).

yet rather unprepossessing house opened directly on to the road. Behind, lay a moat, possibly a diversion of the Bear Brook, and a park-like garden. In summer, the garden was often made available for parties and picnics for guides, brownies and even Sunday school classes. Opposite to it, there was a dark little house turned into offices and occupied by Stanley Wilkins and Son (Solicitors). Sometimes, the smell of brewing pervaded the area, for near at hand was Aylesbury Brewery Company, its plants still operated by steam coal as its chimneys belied. The coal was conveniently delivered from the basin of the canal which lay nearby and to which barges, some still drawn by horses, arrived from the main Grand Union system. To the same part of the street belonged the Baptist chapel, about which tales were told of unusual christenings.

Somewhere in this neighbourhood, the parish of Aylesbury ended and that of Walton began. It was suggested that the reedy little Bear Brook was the boundary. (Naturally, children wondered why it was called the "Bear" Brook.) Anyway, Walton was said to be an old parish and one expected another St Mary's church at its centre. Instead there was a rather unpretentious flint church. Beyond lay another of Aylesbury's pavements which excited the interest of children. It was elevated above the road and had a protective rail. Stepped up from it were three attractive Regency houses, the balconied home of the Parsons family and the stuccoed residence of the Otway Maynes with its monkey puzzle tree. Otway Mayne was a sufficiently strange name to stick in the memory. The elevated pavement continued round into Walton Road. Walton Road broke into leafiness behind an unusual pond, half-railed, half-overgrown with weeds. The pleasant Read home lay on the far side of the pond. Nice old Walton Grange, with its tall trees and fields, lent a rural air to the road. As the home of the Hazells, it was but a stone's throw away from the big Printing Works which marked the end of the High Street.

While the odour of hops hung around the middle reaches of Walton Street, a faint smell of coal gas always lingered around the lower reaches of High Street. Here, the gas plant and the gas holder stood beside the branch line of the London Midland and Scottish Railway. The station premises were already somewhat down at heel and the rolling stock was beginning to look antique. A small

Fig. 16. The Viney House.

engine drew two or three carriages to Cheddington, with a gated
halt at Marston Gate. Occasionally, a train went all the way to
Bletchley. There was a signal box at Park Street level crossing.
Livestock was also transported for the cattle market off Exchange
Street. Between the railway and the canal there was an extensive
area of low-lying land, sometimes flooded by the Bear Brook,
from which osiers were harvested to supply a basket factory on
Park Street.

Gas of a different kind was dispensed by High Street's dentists.
One had a receptionist and an unwelcoming waiting-room. The
other is remembered for the fine lace curtains that hung in the
front windows. In High Street, more comfortable entertainment
was provided than in the Town Hall. The privately-built Pavilion
Cinema was presided over by Mrs Senior herself (drop earrings
again). Usherettes with flashing torches led the way to the seats. A
solemn commissionaire paced down the aisle to draw the curtains
that covered the screen. Miss Samms, the pianist, followed with
her sheaf of music. At the matinees on Wednesdays and Saturdays,
tea was served to the patrons of the balcony. Little trays held a
teapot and small cakes. There was the inevitable clatter of their
collection as soon as the "big picture" started.

High Street juxtaposed upmarket and downmarket clothing
stores. Opposite the Pavilion was Florrie Harper's modish hat shop,
with models for all occasions. Next door was Madame Bates with
perhaps a couple of unpriced hats and a single dress in the window,
all anticipating the Ascot race meeting or some such event. Mr
Kingham (Bertie), with a wart on nose and a waddling dog, the
object of schoolboy amusement, lived in the ivy-clad house next
door. It is doubtful if either of these shops registered with him –
or, for that matter, Longley's, the largest of the upmarket clothing
shops. Here, men's clothing was made to measure: little could be
bought off the peg. Two doors away everything was off the peg
at Hermon's. Mens' wear and working wear took to the pavement
– coats and raincoats, boiler suits and overalls, trousers, breeches
and knickerbockers. The narrow shop was crammed up to the
ceiling with boxes of underwear, shirts and socks. It was possible
to buy a cap for sixpence. The shop had a sort of cotton, woolly,

g. 17. A map of High Street with its railway terminal and gas plant (reproduced from the
925 OS Map).

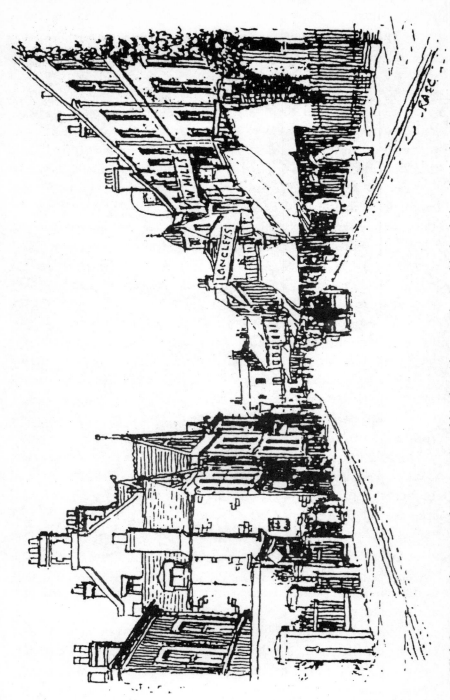

Fig. 18. High Street as such was scarcely a generation old in the mid-1920s. The Canal had only been bridged in the 1890s.

frowsty smell. Near at hand was Narbeth's, a much bigger shop for bargains in women's clothes and household goods, not excluding haberdashery. High Street also enjoyed an expert women's tailoress at Jarvis's. Next door were the Misses Spragg, specialists in children's clothes (we always wanted to attach antlers to the ladies and call them Stagg). Middleton's, across the street, sold yet more haberdashery and a great range of what were described as "unmentionables". Among them were garments which could be obtained less expensively than those obtained discreetly by way of the "Spirella lady", who paid private visits to her customers with a little black attaché case.

As a shopping street, High Street is also remembered for the cakes and confectionery of Ritchings. There was always a tiered wedding cake in the window (Was it ever sold? Did it never go stale?). Dukes's, the watch repairers and jewellers, was presided over by little Mr Dukes (very tall Mrs Dukes, his consort). Allen's fruit and vegetables spilled its cornucopia on to the street. Janes's fish shop was also open-fronted. Invariably, there was a wonderful display of fish on the marble slab from which the melting ice dripped. Plaice and sole, halibut and turbot were most commonly bought for consumption. There were herring and sprats in season – even oysters. In season, there was the sight of salmon, even trout. Cod was for cats.

Waters's unusual semicircle of a shop at the top of the street always seemed more interesting than their main shop because of its shape. Thrasher's, men's outfitters, was owned by a man who bore the title Alderman ("What is an alderman?"). Then there was Milburne's photographic studio. The photographer used a box plate camera, covered his head with a black cloth and called for a static pose. Small scenic backdrops and a selection of furniture stood around the studio. It must have been the same since the turn of the century.

Looking down the High Street, Hazell, Watson and Viney's printing works and Nestlé's condensed milk factory rose up, beyond them the line of the Chiltern Hills. Hazell, Watson and Viney's factory is a memory of machines which whirred and clattered night and day ("What is a night shift?"). Nestlé's disappointed because it was only a milk depot and did not produce chocolates. Nevertheless, it had a marvellously tall chimney on Park Street overlooking the canal.

The canal towpath was forbidden territory. It was associated with drownings, suicides and undesirable people. Dismay was expressed at the occasional swimmer who took to the water ("Cats are drowned there and there's no telling what is thrown overboard from barges"). But there is a memory of a hard and snowy winter when, save near the locks, skaters risked the ice and were reputed to have gone all the way to the main canal at Marsworth. Meanwhile, the boat people were sealed in the Walton Street basin, the chimney pipes from their stoves smoking ceaselessly.

VIII

GOING TO SCHOOL

There is no memory of the first day at school, but I suspect that there were problems subsequently. The walk to school was by way of Kingsbury and Pebble Lane. A tall iron pump in the wall fascinated me. Opposite, on the brick wall of what had formerly been a school, there were the marks left by pupils where they had sharpened their slate pencils. St Mary's passage beside the museum led to the preparatory class of Temple School in Church Street. There was a zinc-roofed hut, with an erratic coke stove and a small playground behind a high wooden gate. The school was presided over by a solitary mistress, Miss Wills, who was sometimes supported by a Miss Beryl who seemed to have a perpetual cold. Miss Wills had an eagle eye behind steel rimmed spectacles. She looked most at home in her guide uniform. We always wondered what the lanyard and whistle were for. In winter, if the coke stove declined to produce as much heat as was required, the arithmetic class took to the playground, where tables were chanted vigorously in unison and feet were stamped and hands were clapped rhythmically.

It must have been here that the earliest reading and writing lessons were given. The first books that made an impression were the volumes of Arthur Mee's *Children's Encyclopedia*. Its pictures stick clearly in the mind. There was a romantic scene from *A Midsummer Night's Dream*, complete with Oberon, Titania, Puck and Bully Bottom with the ass's head. The captions of two other illustrations must have been among the first words that I was able to read, because they remain so clearly. One was, "Will the Ice Age come again?" This was beneath a picture of an eskimo building an igloo. The other caption was, "How will the world end?" beneath a picture of a galaxy.

And, so it was, to lie in bed and look at the night sky – for the bedroom curtains were never drawn – was to wonder about the stars. They were known to have names – Mars and Venus were probably the first to be identified. A more interesting name was

Jack-and-his-plough, but he disappeared all too easily among the multitude of stars until one searched diligently for him. The Milky Way was an intriguing name never fully appreciated. Anyway, to be in bed and focus upon a single bright star was to sense it growing bigger and to be concerned that it was on its way to collide with the earth.

The moon also cast its light through the window and its rays kept you awake. It was known to have all sorts of shapes from week to week and to disappear altogether for short periods. It could also sometimes appear dangerously large on the horizon and to turn red as though something awful was happening to it.

The upper school, for which a new building containing three classrooms and other facilities was erected in New Street, lost its boys at the age of ten. There were memorable history lessons. The dates of crowned heads of England were recited round the class weekly. Indeed, one sat in a seat named after a monarch. The seats of William the Conqueror and George V were most coveted. To make a mistake when the name of your Monarch was requested was to be sent down a seat in the line of succession. The staff included tall Miss Irene who reminded us of a stork; attractive Miss Greenland who always wore a gym slip: a French mademoiselle who wooed children to her language from the age of nine with a pack of Happy Family cards; and Miss Amery herself who taught advanced maths – she was the first to utter the word *geometry*. Folk dancing was encouraged. Plimsolls were worn out rehearsing *Rufty Tufty*, *Roger de Coverley*, and *Sellinger's Round* for the annual parents' day. A genial Mr Timothy came on Tuesdays to give music lessons (taff-a-tiffy, taff-a-tiffy) on an upright piano in a room in which lingered a smell of stale toast. Sometimes, Miss Gleaves in much knitwear sat before a one bar electric fire to pronounce upon a pupil's progress.

Schools in Aylesbury were divided into those where the pupils wore caps (hats for the girls) and those where they went bareheaded. (How could you greet an adult properly if there was no cap to raise?) Those in the two church schools went capless, but they maintained a good reputation. St Mary's school was a long way off down the Oxford Road. It was renowned for the standing of its headmaster who was also choirmaster at St Mary's church. Everything that was good about a schoolmaster was said about him. St John's school, behind the red brick church in Cambridge Street, was dominated by two whitehaired old ladies, never without hats and gloves. It sounded as though it was a happy school. The playground was alive with skipping children. From these schools, older pupils usually went to the Queen's Park schools which were light and airy with large asphalt playgrounds, though never the sign of a sports field.

To transfer from Temple School to the twenty-year-old building of the mixed Grammar School was a major experience, though the transfer took place in the company of friends. Dark blue and light blue caps had to yield to red and black caps. Football boots for winter and blazers for summer had to be acquired. Some three hundred pupils filled the premises; there were separate entrances for boys and girls. Classrooms were crowded. There was a large house for the head master. Most of the staff lived within walking or cycling distance. There is no distinct memory of any having a car. Until the first bicycle was obtained, it was necessary to stay to lunch. The meal took place in a wooden hut which also served as a setting for cookery classes. The hut always had the smell of some previous meal. Memories are of interminable overcooked New Zealand "lamb", with boiled cabbages in winter, stringy beans in summer with thick dark brown gravy of uncertain provenance. There might follow milk pudding with a spoonful of jam, steamed puddings with a gluey sauce or pies with hard crusts covered with thin custard. Drinking water was always warm.

New pupils were immediately allotted to houses – an arbitrary business. Homework entered the scene. Music lessons, which consisted principally of singing traditional songs, offered light relief partly because an increasing number of voices began to break. Budding clowns broke into piercing falsetto. The tolerant music master also taught geography. He had travelled widely as a naval officer during the First World War. Geography, it was rapidly discovered, was a matter of "casting a circle round the globe in forty minutes". It was good to have pointed out the reasons for the different forms of the land in the Vale – the soft chalk of the

Chilterns to the south and the harder limestone hills to the north. (Whitchurch boys were asked about the stone buildings and walls in their village). The sandy outcrops of the Wing area were contrasted with the sticky clays in the Vale, where a host of little streams joined together to feed the River Thame. And, for the first time, the heights of different areas in the Vale above sea level were revealed.

The weekly drawing class was anything but inspiring for children. A circular metal rail was erected in the school hall. In its centre on a low table, there would be an arrangement of cubes, cones and cylinders. With paper attached to drawing boards and seated uncomfortably on chairs, attempts had to be made to make a drawing of the model. In conjunction with this the drawing master enunciated very slowly "the principles of perspective". Mr Buckingham, who was probably something of an artist himself, wore a knickerbocker suit, heavy boots and, throughout the class, a tweed hat. It was more than evident that he chewed tobacco. Could he have been on some sort of wavelength with Cézanne who, only a year or two earlier, had written in a letter, "Everything in nature is formed after the sphere, the cone and the cylinder"? At least he turned to nature for homework with water colours for flowers or autumn leaves. They were always "common" flowers – "the common poppy", "the common buttercup", "the common daffodil".

And so to botany, made the more attractive by one appealing teacher. There was an innate personal attraction to plants and flowers, perhaps something inbred.[8] Wildflowers were associated with some of the earliest recollections – blowing away dandelion seeds, holding buttercups under the chin, avoiding making daisy chains, playing with the clinging goosegrass. Seeds also fascinated – shaken from pods and flower heads, parachuted from thistle heads. The shapes of leaves fascinated, especially with their autumn colouring. All climbers that covered walls were called Virginia creepers, until an appealing new name was introduced – Ampelopsis (another of those words which became a fun word). Mosses and lichens had an early appeal. It was exciting to learn that plants had Latin names – Christian names and family names. Many were to stick and replace popular names. *Caltha palustris* was to be remembered ahead of Marsh Marigold.[9] And the family names became increasingly familiar – *Rosaceae, Cruciferae, Ranunculaceae, Umbeliferae. Umbeliferae* was a jolly word. (It was not long before a person was called "an umbel", a word that no one would understand – relished as a secret constituent in a childhood vocabulary).

And the name of Linnaeus was introduced and a *Flora* had to be purchased (another book to be put on the parental account). And the names of the parts of plants had to be learned. Flowers were dissected.[10] Big new botanical words were learned – monocotyledon and dicotyledon. The quality of the surface of leaves and stems introduced the word *glabrous*. (Just at the time that "Jabberwocky" turned up in poetry lessons). Immediately "the slythy tove" became "glabrous". Aromatic (another new adjective) plants, crushed and smelt, were rapidly identified by name – all the herbs in the garden. On Sunday walks in autumn the hedgerow fruits were identified. The berries of the hawthorn (haws) were sometimes called "birds' bread and cheese". The rose hip was known to be used for a kind of marmalade. The bitter sloe contorted the mouth. The crab apple was picked for jelly; elderberries for wine. There was the taste of honey at the end of the long corolla tube of the honeysuckle. In certain hedges there were to be found wild plums (or bullases). And there were colourful poison berries – those of the woody nightshade and the bryony.

Botanical walks from school were much enjoyed. To stand in a green meadow and to begin to identify one or two of the "more than a hundred different kinds of grasses", was a revelation. And, although wheat, barley and oats were already recognised by name, it was at school it was learned that they were members of Natural Order Graminae. (Rye was first encountered on August Bank Holiday at Stewkley – taller than an eleven-year-old).

There was one unforgettable botanical walk from school along the canal footpath. "Today we will identify weeds" (what an enlightened challenge). There was the familiar stinging nettle ("It can be eaten when young like spinach"). White and red dead nettles did not sting. Jack-by-the-hedge was to be recognised by its garlic smell and the ragged robin by its pungent odour when crushed.

The young leaves of the dandelion could be eaten when crushed ("Taste one"). And on the other side of the tow path, there were the plants (still weeds) that grew in the water – reeds and rushes. And a root was pulled up and called a "rhizome" – another new word.

Knowledge about trees was absorbed rather more on Sunday walks than at school. Some were identified by their seeds – the acorns from the long line of oaks down Buckingham Road, the horse chestnuts on Bierton Road. There were "spinners", the winged seeds, of the English maple – widely distributed by the wind. Beech nuts were collected at Wendover. Fir cones were less easy to find. There were two monkey puzzle trees – one in High Street, the other in Walton Street. We were told that they were also pine trees. Of course, there was familiarity with hazel nuts (cob nuts) from autumn walks. And there were friends who had a walnut tree.

And because plants belonged to families that had names, it did not seem strange to learn that different fruits had names. Apples came in different varieties. Cox's Orange Pippin was the first name to be learned. The cherries in the Chilterns were also known by name before going to the Grammar School, with white hearts the favourite.

There being no zoology at school, the names of birds in particular, were picked up in the course of a rural upbringing. And the natives as well as the seasonal visitors had their names mentioned by boys in the classroom because of their eggs. It was not unusual for the fragile blown eggs to be brought for exchange in small boxes lined with cotton wool.

The physics lab (also a chemistry lab) is remembered for the lingering smell of Bunsen burners. The woodwork shed – a World War I timber building purchased from the Ministry of Defence, had a distinct smell of sawdust and wood shavings. There was little attraction in the first task. An inch square foot rule had to be produced out of a chunk of wood. Nor did the playing field exactly excite – the more so when a part of the games period might be spent with spades and wheelbarrows trying to smooth out the ridged and furrowed grassland.

Mathematics changed its form, as well as the French language. Arithmetic seemed to multiply and divide itself into geometry and algebra (trigonometry, too, at a later stage). And there emerged things called equations, where the letters of the alphabet were mixed up with mathematical signs. Meanwhile, to the simple and appealing conversational French enjoyed at the junior school with the French mademoiselle, were overruled by grammar and irregular verbs, let alone the complications of the feminine and the masculine. Yet, for some reason, while there was a revolt at the mathematical complications, there was no similar reaction to the changing character of French language lessons.

The school hall served many functions – from morning assembly to evening entertainment. The first Empire Day celebration is recalled, the member countries being represented by pupils dressed in appropriate costumes and carrying the relevant flags. The hornpipe was danced in sailor costumes. The hall was also used as a gymnasium and there was some excitement when structures called parallel bars were erected. There were three ropes suspended from somewhere in the ceiling and which were used for climbing. Thick dusty mats were brought out on which somersaults and handstands were practised. An apparatus over which vaulting was practised had difficulty in finding a home. And surveying all of these activities from a high point on the wall was an original portrait of the illustrious founder of the school, Sir Henry Lee of Ditchley.[11]

IX

GOING FOR A WALK

Everybody went for walks. A walk was supposed to be good for you – something called "a constitutional". It was expected to be a source of pleasure. One walked *down* Bicester Road, *down* Buckingham Road, *down* Hartwell Road and *up* Bierton Road. Tring Road, Wendover Road and Old Stoke Road (as it was called) were too far away.

Going for a walk often implied stopping to talk. It was unusual to encounter someone who did not wish to pass the time of day. The opening courtesies were generally about the weather and its seasonableness. There might be presumed a need for rain (a dry spell, a good shower, a mild spell) or for a frost (to kill the germs or pests in the garden). The wind was a good topic ("enough to do this to you" . . . "enough to do that to you" . . .). The phases of the moon – new moon, old moon, harvest moon . . . could extend the conversation. If autumn seemed to set in too early, "St Luke's little summer" was forecast comfortingly. Fog eliminated the prospect of a walk. It was unhealthily damp. February was "fill dyke". Blackthorn in bloom presaged cold weather – the "Blackthorn winter". March winds blew dust from the fields with lighter soil.

The walk *down* the Bicester Road passed by the homes of a number of friends and acquaintances. There was the new nurses' home, the residence of a friendly bank clerk, the double-fronted house of a prosperous building merchant, the home of the best-known teacher of shorthand and typing (with a monkey puzzle tree in the garden next door). There were the homes of a sprinkling of tradespeople whose accommodation over their shops was too cramped and of two people who were referred to as "tallymen" (a "profession" which sounded strange in the ears of children). Beyond an alderman's overgrown garden, there was a row of artisans' cottages with long front gardens. Then came a public house which had the happy name of *The Hop Pole* (hops being unknown to children, it was assumed to be some kind of a pole on which one hopped). A private road beside the public house led to the factory where Cubitt cars were made. The Cubitt was a quality car of the day and the open tourer was much esteemed locally. It was thought that it would make Aylesbury a second Cowley. Northern Road was the home of the Aylesbury Steam Laundry (and we used to ask "Why steam?"). Opposite to Northern Road was the Dominion Dairy, home of Golden Acres butter – which local inhabitants knew to be New Zealand butter arriving in large square boxes (called butter boxes). The imported butter was reprocessed to make it more spreadable and presented as a product of the dairy herds of the Vale of Aylesbury. The Dominion Dairy also produced a less-successful line of silver-wrapped processed cheese portions. Beyond the factory were more allotments and the clinkered road down which it was forbidden to go because it led to the sewage works. At the top of Hayden Hill the chief of police lived in a staid brick house next to which there was a rather pretentious dairy that advertised The Hadley Herd. Between them ran a gated road through several fields to Cold Harbour Farm. It was a strange name and no one could explain it. The descent to the flood plain of the River Thame led to a concrete bridge which was eventually to be decorated with Aylesbury's coat of arms.

A flood plain is for flooding. In most years for most of the winter, hundreds of acres alongside the River Thame were covered with shallow water. Frost was accordingly awaited keenly. It made skating permissible because the shallow waters froze easily and only wet feet were suffered if the ice gave way. In summer what passed for the boat of a friend might be rowed for a few yards along the river before it got stuck in the reeds and waterweed. Footpaths beyond the river made their way to Quarrendon ruins.[12] It was a disappointing sight. There was no more than a solitary stone arch crumbling into a jungle of thorn bushes, brambles and nettles. But it was a legendary place – all that was left of the colourful property of Sir Henry Lee, who was subsequently promoted to Oxford's Ditchley Park. Part of the old Quarrendon domain was occupied by the Terry Farm – Berryfields, as it was called. It was the home of a family much given to following the Whaddon Chase fox hounds. There were always horses and foals in the surrounding fields.

Hartwell Road offered the most appealing of the walks. Beyond the rather mean Whitehall Street, the road descended down to what (to us) was a steep little hill overhung with trees and flanked by two walled gardens. On the left, the Prebendal garden had some of the earliest snowdrops in spring. On the right, was the Gate House, its entrance through a big gloomy gate A little further on were several down-at-heel cottages outside which laundry flapped. Interest began with Collier's mill at the meeting point of two streams. One stream ran swiftly to the mill race beneath a three-storey building. The mill was said to be very old, though incorporated in the brickwork was the date 1892 plain for all to see.

Beyond the mill and the railway bridge where, on a lucky day, there might be an enveloping swirl of smoke and steam, lay meadows, two small streams and yet another allotment. Then the vista of Hartwell Park opened up, with a footpath to the right of the Star Lodge. The path passed through fields with roundels of chestnut trees and herds of cattle. In summer, shoes became covered with "buttercup dust". Grasshoppers could be caught and darting dragonflies seen. Later in the season horseflies were a nuisance and sent the cattle gadding. Molehills and ant-heaps were prodded vainly in the hope of disturbing the occupants. The footpath led by a reedy lake edged with figwort and marsh marigolds which gave way to arrowheads and water buttercups. The bulrushes were naturally linked with Moses in Egypt. Sometimes there were swans to be seen and fluffy cygnets. There were always moorhens, sometimes with their young.

The wooded road at the end of the footpath led to Lower Hartwell and the mossy, mysterious Egyptian Springs. A stone shelter with hieroglyphs across its arch drew the eyes from the dark stone seat and fungus around its supports. The springs bubbled away in a stone trough on the opposite side of the road. At Hartwell, it was said that nightingales could be heard on summer evenings. Certainly the coarse cries of the pheasants and the first cuckoos could be heard there. Hartwell House was invisible; so, too, its walled kitchen garden. But the Gothic chapel at the entrance to the drive never ceased to attract attention.[13]

To the left of Star Lodge, the footpath was raised above the level of the road. Would-be springs oozed into a ditch after heavy rains and sappy forget-me-nots enjoyed the moisture. A seat on which tramps not infrequently sat – trekking from the Poor Law Institution at Aylesbury to that at Thame – was sheltered by a spreading yew tree. Behind it were the clay pits of a disused brickyard. Violets were to be found in the hedgerow in spring. Winding its way around the Hartwell property there was a long wall of Oolitic limestone. The wall stirred the imagination because of the curiously fossilised stones and occasional ammonites that were set in it. It was told that ammonites were sometimes called snake stones – from their shape like a curled-up snake. As children we had our own name for them. We christened them "whirligig stones". There was also a glimpse through the lodge gates of a column with a statue on top. The road took a sharp turn at the Bugle Horn hotel, with its colourful summer garden. The village of Stone beyond introduced a different sort of countryside. A panorama opened up towards Eythorpe and the hills of Waddesdon and Winchendon. There are also vague memories of fields where there were strongly scented cowslips, occasional orchids and lady-smocks which flagged and sagged before they could be brought home. There were certainly fritillaries, subsequently banished to the bank of ditches by wartime ploughing and never to return to the rotational grassland that followed. Further along the Stone road, there were wooden signs pointing to places with foreign-sounding names – Haddenham, Cuddington and Worminghall. They were all part of the romance of the Hartwell walk.

Buckingham road began much the same as Bicester road. Here there was a row of substantial two-storeyed houses facing the raised pavement. They mostly had cellars with windows peeping out below the front door steps. Their gardens backed on to a cindered lane. Between them and the string of artisans' collages of varying character, was Willow Road – without a willow in sight – and muddy, rutted Dunsham Lane. The lane was the regular haunt of gypsy encampments, but it was good for blackberrying. Allotments lay behind the elm and hawthorn hedges, with the usual cluster of untidy sheds. The isolated Horse and Jockey was the last building before the little River Thame. It was an interestingly old building, but somewhat neglected. Holman's bridge over the river prompted

Fig. 19. The Egyptian Spring at Hartwell. The feature has been restored to its original state.

the question, "Who was Holman?" The river was half-choked with reeds, its banks lined with the holes of water rats. The distinctive road to Whitchurch was described as a "turnpike" road. It had wide grass verges and a long line of oaks on the east side, beneath which acorns were to be collected. A Civil War battle was ascribed to the vicinity. It raised false hopes that a canonball or a fragment of armour might be found.

Bierton Road, the Aylesbury end of the Leighton Buzzard Turnpike, took off from the curiously nondescript Cambridge Street. At the town end, its one-up-and-one-down cottages were dominated by the brick bastion of St John's church (a place of childhood interest because "they burnt incense there"). Near at hand was a fish shop, the owner of which ran a "fish round" in his pony and trap. There was also an Off-licence shop ("Off-licence" needed to be explained) and a rough field where fairs sometimes were held. Beyond Park Street (again, no park), the road began to rise, with Manor Park flanking the northern side. Up the hill, the houses stood in pairs, facing the walled garden of Manor House.[14] Among them was Vulcan House, where the maternal grandparents lived. The house carries no memories other than that of a wedding reception, of powerfully scented Philadelphus (called orange-blossom) and summer bees. All the houses had stone window and door surrounds. No one seemed to know where all the stone came from.

At the top of Bierton Hill two formidable buildings faced each other — the prison and the workhouse. The stern classical façade of the women's gaol, its heavy main gate and high walls made an unpleasant impact. In the railed bosky gardens of the administrative homes, there were tennis courts where we sometimes played. The Poor Law Institution, with its leaded diamond-shaped window panes, its trim front gardens with their box-hedge parterres made a contrasting impression. Lord Carrington's name appeared on the wooden notice board at the entrance to the allotments. Several solitary houses punctuated the road to Bierton. Near the entrance to one of them was an ancient elm tree from which it was claimed men were hanged. To the south, beyond the hedgerows, the outline of the Chiltern Hills stretched as far as the eye could see. Several footpaths took off on either side of the road, passing through stinging nettles, though there were always dock leaves available to ease the stings. The fine old Bierton church commanded the entrance to the village, with its several scores of period houses and cottages. Bierton was renowned as the nearest village to have a "rat and sparrow" club, the members of which received a pecuniary reward for all the rat's tails and sparrow's heads that they could muster.

Cambridge Street itself is remembered for Millburn's auction rooms at the Buckingham Street intersection. It was a lively scene on most Saturday mornings. Farther down was Sanford's, the cycle shop, behind which grew an ancient mulberry tree from which the first mulberries were tasted. It was intriguing to pass through Narbeth's shop opposite to it, into the High Street. Close to New Street stood a murky little shop run by a portly, unshaven but sympathetic owner rejoicing in the name of Stegall. He was a purveyor of everything appertaining to the wireless (which had not yet become the radio) — aerials, tubes, bulbs, wires, "cat's whiskers". His cramped premises were the haunt of all who owned a crystal set. His shop faced Upper Hundreds, together with Hale Leys, perhaps Aylesbury's most interesting name for the young.

Upper Hundreds was a fast developing slum. So, too, was Malden Terrace which ran parallel with Cambridge Street off New Street.

New Street was a kind of back Buckingham Street and about a third of it had garden walls which marked the end of Buckingham Street gardens. It is remembered as a brickish street (as G. M. Hopkins might have expressed it). Short cul-du-sacs of terraced houses led off it into fields – Alexander Terrace, Havelock Street, Fleet Street. Fleet Street contained the Zenana Mission Hut (memories of a Sunday School tea-party in its garden with egg-and-spoon races). 37, Buckingham Street had no garden, but a detached part of Cannon's Buckingham Street garden was rented. Its four walls were covered with espaliered fruit trees and there was a summer house off which pink paint was peeling. There was a chicken run and two rabbits were kept in a chicken wire enclosure out of which they enjoyed burrowing. In one corner there was an inexplicable mound of oyster shells. Going to the garden one morning there was a strange sight. For about fifty yards, the entire road and pavements of New Street were covered in a layer of straw, to deaden the sound of passing traffic and to let people know that there was someone who was very ill in a bedroom fronting on the street. Somewhere in New Street there lived a sweep. There was also a cobbler, with dark squinting eyes, a black trilby hat, steel-rimmed spectacles and black fingernails.

Going for a walk had an aim – or, more correctly, was given a nominal aim. It might be to see if Mr So-and-so had finished this or that to his home or garden, to see if a certain farmer had completed his haymaking, harvesting or ploughing and sowing. Seasonally, one went to hear the larks as they climbed up from the ploughed fields, to look out for the first lambs, swifts and swallows. In the autumn, the purpose might be to pick colourful leaves (which seemed to lose their lustre as soon as they were brought indoors) and berries (none of which retained the incandescent glow that they displayed in the hedgerow). The bright polish on the horse chestnuts became dull overnight. Autumn walks might offer the excitement of a startled pheasant as it flew lumberingly over the hedge – more rarely the scuttle of a handful of partridges before they whirred in flight.

Seasonally, all sorts of nouns were converted into verbs on going for a walk. One went birdsnesting, blackberrying, mushrooming, dandelioning (on Dandelion Sunday for making dandelion wine). It was possible to go elderberrying in September, but though they might make a white wine, one never went "elderflowering" – or, for that matter, "crabappling" (for jelly) or "sloeing" (in anticipation of sloe gin).

Going for a walk meant "keeping a weather eye open", for there were no reliable forecasts on the wireless even if one listened to them. The behaviour and patterns of the clouds had to be observed. Old jingles were regularly quoted. A red sky in the morning really seemed to mean rain. If it rained before seven it really did seem to shine before eleven. None of the walks offered much shelter against even a shower. It soon became clear that umbrellas only made you think you were keeping dry because no rain fell on your face. In winter, east winds had a habit of chapping the legs and clothes might even seem to go stiff with the cold.

Other people went on walks too. None of them failed to pass the time of day. Walking sticks were swung rhythmically – nobbled ash rivalling polished hardwood, silver ringed and neatly ferruled. Many wanted to stop and gossip (irksome for children). Bowler hats, trilby hats, and caps were raised to all and sundry. Socks had a habit of wriggling down into shoes ("Pull your socks up").

It was on walks that one learned the names of things. To the vocabulary of plants was added that of animals. Cows and bulls were refined into heifers and bullocks – and slowly into familiar breeds – Ayrshires, Shorthorns, Jerseys, Guernseys. Named breeds of sheep followed suit ("Watch out for rams if you are crossing a field, where there is a flock of sheep"). No one seemed to be able to reply to a childish question – "Why do animals grazing in a field all seem to point their heads in the same direction?"

Going for a walk was usually a pleasant experience, but around Aylesbury, it would have been much nicer if the roads had meandered a little and had not been so uninterestingly straight. It would have been better still if one had not always had to walk *back*.

X

FARTHER AFIELD

In the 1920s, the Vale of Aylesbury influenced the town more than the town influenced the Vale. The town was a focus for the countryfolk. Townsfolk did not often travel much beyond the horseshoe of the hills – chequered with fields to the north; half-wooded to the south – that defined the Vale on three sides. Only a minority went to distant places for "summer holidays". Not many more paid regular visits to London by rail. The geographical experience of most was very limited.

The Vale was not a dramatic piece of country. Its tributary streams were gathered into the River Thame which (one learned) flowed west into the Thames. But that was in Oxfordshire, foreign territory. To traverse the height of land that separated the drainage basins of the Thames and Ouse was to trespass into another county called Bedfordshire. For those who lived within its confines, the Vale could probably be summed up in the words of Gerard de Nerval about his home area in France – "a land of golden mean, of modest charm". By the 1920s, the gold might have lost something of its glitter. The charm had probably been more evident in the days before the decline of farming which had led to the neglect of hedgerows and fences, to tumbledown gates and overgrown ditches and to the widespread employment of cheap barbed wire.

The farmers of the Vale, dealers apart, generally had an allegiance to one auctioneer and one market. There were, of course, some who lived midway between Aylesbury and other market towns – Winslow, Leighton Buzzard, Thame, Buckingham, Bicester, Tring, most of which were ten miles or so away. Six miles was about the most that animals travelled comfortably on the hoof to market. For dairy cows there was the need to relate walking time to milking time. It was not unusual to see milk dripping from cows as they returned from market. Ice and snow prohibited movement and were likely to lead to the closure of local markets. Wooden signposts pointed the way. Weather-worn milestones stepped out the distance, newer iron markers filling any gaps. In winter, there was anxiety about arriving at the home farm before dark.

The people of Aylesbury mostly had their roots in the Vale. Immigrants to the town came principally from the surrounding countryside. Others remained "foreigners" for at least a generation. Emigrants from the town were usually deemed to have left "to better themselves". Some did; some were known not to. The days of apprenticeship had largely expired, save in some trade-unionised activities. Apprenticeship was reputed to be very strict in the printing industry. Advertisements for "hands" were still made, with boys and strong lads wanted for all sorts of casual labour. Probably half of the houses in Buckingham Street had a housemaid living-in. There seemed to be wholes armies of cleaners, of part-time cooks, of jobbing gardeners and handymen, and of launderers who took in washing. There were also nurses who came in case of illness – Nurse Figg came to look after us. The nurses also acted as midwives and were normally called to lay out the deceased.

In many if not most families, aunts and uncles were numbered in double figures. There were six uncles and one aunt in my father's family – another boy having died in childhood. In my mother's family, there were two aunts and two uncles. Cousins were beginning to dwindle in number. There was still something of the extended family to be observed. This was absolutely the case at times of funerals.

To travel into the countryside was also to journey into territory where the local accent was increasingly pronounced. To the north and east of the Vale in particular, the glottal stop was employed with vigour and there was a distinct Anglo-Saxon legacy in the dialect. With hindsight, it could be argued that in and around the family farm at Stewkley it was a legacy from the days of the original settlement. The place-name is Anglo-Saxon and the settlement lay on the frontiers of the Danelaw. Traces of sounds familiar in north-east Buckinghamshire can be recognised in the Jutish peninsula. Villages such as Stewkley experienced little population mobility. They displayed a steady outflow of population typical of an agricultural community. There was no reason why

Fig. 20. Stewkley Church. Its architectural qualities were unappreciated at the time. There is a fine drawing of the distinctive Norman features in Kenneth and Margaret Morley, op.cit., p.43.

those who remained in the village should change their speech patterns and accents, let alone their vocabularies. With little population mobility, there was also considerable intermarriage among the village families, though as a warning against it, there was posted in the church porch the table of relations with which wedlock was proscribed. The village had six or seven extended families which bore common names, but which appeared to have no consanguinity. In the village, there were many who had remarkably similar facial features and expressions, but who had no known family relationship.[15] The first William Mead to be recorded in Stewkley was born in 1538. Those he begat (a word taken up by children in a jokey way) within two generations were to be found in London. The name William was to dominate the males in the family for half a millennium.

Church Farm at Stewkley was visited four or five times a year. It seemed a long journey in the confined space of an old Ford taxi which was run by a war veteran from the village. There were plenty of twists and turns on the road – Hulcott (no through road), Rowsham (the brewery was always mentioned), Wingrave crossroads (very dangerous), Wing Hill, Mentmore Park off to the right, Cublington turn, eventually "the longest village in Bucks". It was "Stewkley, God help us" to neighbouring villagers. Church Farm, as its name implied, stood next to the stern and solid church. The church, with the brick built village school opposite to it, divided the settlement into "uptown" and "downtown". The church is remembered as feeling rather cold, even in summer, and smelling rather musty. The south face was warmed by sunshine, but its stone arch incorporated unpleasant bird-like heads. Its ring of bells was cheerful, save for the so-called "ting, tang" which rang commandingly for the last five minutes to summon likely late-comers. A gloomy drive led to the Victorian vicarage. It was said to be haunted by the ghost of one Wadley.

The farmhouse consisted of three linked parts. There was a double-fronted early Victorian section – up one step with a steeply rising staircase behind the front door. A low-ceilinged, brick-floored dairy, divided into two parts, lay behind. The structure of the loft above and its three leaded windows suggested that it was of eighteenth-century origin. The third section was probably part of the original dwelling. To enter, adults had to bend their heads. There was a stone-slabbed floor and on the far side, there was a winding staircase every tread of which creaked. It led to a bedroom with two double beds and a somewhat sinister wooden chest. The kitchen had a big open fireplace before which at Christmas and Easter a large Dutch oven was placed. Inside, it had a little mechanical contrivance which was wound up like a clock. On its hook was suspended the inevitable joint of beef which slowly rotated clockwise, then anti-clockwise. A little door in the rear of the oven could be opened to baste the joint. There was no running water in the kitchen, but there was a handpump over a shallow sink. Originally, the pump had been outside the kitchen door, beside a path of cobblestones known as "the pitching". To the rear of the kitchen another door opened on to a bricked yard, always noted for its skiddy surface. Under a shelter was a kind of hand laundry, with a hand-turned mangle. A two-seater privy backed on to the cart shed and a row of stables. Different parts of the house could be identified by their smell. There was the slightly sour smell of cream settling in the leaden pans before it was churned. The neglected front room always had a musty smell. There must have been mothballs in the clothes cupboard. Lamps were inseparable from the smell of paraffin.

The entire house seemed to be riddled with draughts in winter, no matter how blazing were the fires and how heavily curtained were the doors and windows. In particular, draughts emanated from the cupboards on either side of the fireplaces, where the cracks between the floorboards admitted currents of cold air. The dining-room fire was much sought after by the cats and, at Easter time, by the inevitable pet lamb. Light was provided by oil lamps and candles, for the village had no electricity. The warming pan that was pushed up and down the bed was a source of much interest. The chiming grandfather clock was a favourite feature. The barometer was eyed religiously and tapped furtively to see whether it was going up or going down. After listening to a wireless with a loudspeaker at home, it was fascinating to see three headphones put into a large pudding basin so that their combined sound could be better relayed.

At the bottom of the farmyard was a moat and a dank bit of ground that bore the name of "the lower garden". The moat was surrounded by ash and sycamore trees, the seeds of the latter known as "spinners" The garden produced good cabbages, good raspberries and good nettles. Beyond were the farm fields which ended on the other side of a rough lane with a field called "the new bit". (Was it new because it was the last to be purchased or did "bit" derive its name from the Scandinavian "bet" or "beit"?) The rest of the farmland was scattered – the Wing Road fields, the Cricketers' fields and The Ground, which was three or more miles away.

In winter and at Easter, one walked up the Soulbury Road (Soulbury seemed a sad name). At Whitsun, there was a pond in a field called The Slad where newts were to be caught and where the first leech was seen. The newts always escaped from the jars in which they were kept, sometimes in the taxi on the way home (from which they were never recovered). Down the village, on the Cublington Road, was Gallows Hill ("Where they used to hang people"). It was just beyond an uncle's double-fronted house behind which he had worked minor gardening miracles by encouraging mistletoe to grow and had successfully grafted several varieties of apple and pear on to old trees. In summer, the same footpaths were followed annually. The most appealing was that which led to "Hollingden furze". Sometimes it led through a field planted with beans. Once it was sown with an impressive rye crop, the grain nearly five feet high. The land at Hollingden was regarded as poor because it supported gorse. There were exposed ridges of sandy rock into which rabbits burrowed freely.

On the farm, cows were hand-milked. The milk had only recently been collected by lorry, the heavy churns needing to be lifted on to a platform to help the driver. Hay was still made with horsedrawn equipment. Ricks were built and thatched by hand in the farmyard. There was a horse-operated elevator. There was also a strange crop called "latternouth" (a second hay crop?). Grain was still stooked in the field until dry, built into ricks and left until the mobile steam thresher arrived to do its work. The farm dog was much entertained by the mice and rats that ran out of the ricks during the threshing.

In the dairy, butter was made and eggs were laid out for collection by an eggler. Originally, butter was churned from the cream of milk skimmed from the big shallow lead containers that sat on brick supports round the walls of the dairy. The leads (as they were called) had holes through which the skimmed milk was drained into buckets. There was also an Alfa-Laval separator, the handle of which was almost impossible to turn. The machine produced a thin trickle of cream from one spout and a bigger stream of milk from another. The receipts from at least some of the butter had been accumulated in the form of a collection of sovereigns and half-sovereigns. They were husbanded rather than banked.

Wildflowers at Stewkley seemed to be at a premium. At Easter, one went looking for blue and white violets though often in vain. In the grain fields there were plenty of poppies and the occasional cornflower. There is also a memory of a bean field with the never-to-be-forgotten scent of its flowers. Could it have been on the way to an outlying property called Clack? In the same direction the road passed through a shallow ford where there was watercress. We were never there at mushroom time, but those that were brought to town by relatives were much appreciated. Moles were about the only source of interest as far as animals were concerned. Their runs were traced, though there was never any success in digging them out. Moleskins were still sold. They were tacked on to a board and treated with lime. Moleskin coats were still obtainable from furriers and the several acquaintances who wore them were eyed with curiosity.

Near Stewkley was Cottesloe ("Once an important place"). When one of its two farms was visited, it always seemed to be rabbit pie for lunch or fruit pie afterwards. In the eyes of Stewkley folk, the land was said to be poor. The clearest memory is of an airship throbbing its way overhead. Boxing Day return from Stewkley was always after dark and through a countryside without street lamps. The sky was filled with stars ("Why did some twinkle?" No answer.) Another car, headlights dazzling, might be passed between Wing and Aylesbury.

Quite different from Stewkley were the occasional visits to a farm at Quainton. It was probably called "Lower Farm" and was approached across a field. Beside the red brick farmhouse on the other side of a little stream was a garden filled with springtime hyacinths. There was also a double hedgerow which was unusual in that it was carpeted with anemones and primroses. Pussywillow and catkins were also there. Their pollen was described as "nasty dirty stuff" and they were not welcome in the house. Blackthorn and hawthorn blossoms were also refused entry because they were deemed to be unlucky.

Very occasionally, on a light summer evening, there might be a ride in a pony and trap. There are distinct memories of going along the country road from Weedon to Aston Abbots. The gated road through the land of Burston farm was especially appreciated because we were driven off the gated road on to the ridged and furrowed grassland.[16] Up and down the trap went (on what we called "the switchback ride") as the pony's steady trot changed to

an excited little canter. Getting out to open the gate at the Aston
Abbots end it was an additional pleasure to stand on the gate as it
swung to a close. Then the pony would walk up Limes Hill from
where the view would be admired. On the one side there was a
long line of the Chilterns ("Why do they look blue?" No answer).
On the other side, big open ploughed fields stretched to
Whitchurch and beyond.

Wendover was a magical name which was catalogued mentally
with Hartwell. It called for a railway journey, with a steam engine,
a dusty carriage, windows speckled with sooty smuts from the
funnel, motes dancing in the sunbeams. The solitary non-smoking
carriages were always passed over in favour of the normal compartments which, with cigarette butts on the floor, always smelt of
stale tobacco. The journey always brought to mind a poem learned
at school –

> Faster than fairies,
> Faster than witches,
> Bridges and houses,
> Hedges and ditches.[17]

Wendover station had a wooden bridge. It was not as far as it
seemed up the narrow road and footpath that led to the hills. The
distinctive flora always began on the flanks of the railway cutting.
Here, Maytime dog daisies yielded to the scrambling pink ever-
lasting sweet peas of summer, which had only ever been seen
elsewhere in gardens. The footpath was dusty white, sticky after
rain, and it opened up almost immediately to an exposure of
chalk. From this, fragments were chipped off to take home. They
could be used to mark out the hopscotch frame and would even
write on a blackboard.

On the scarp slope it was a matter of learning new plant names.
Wild thyme was easily recognised because it looked like a
diminutive version of the familiar garden variety. Scabious seemed
an unlovely name for an attractive flower. Knapweed's purple
flower appealed, but their stems were unbreakable. Harebells
disappointed because their flowers, like those of bluebells, rapidly
withered when picked. Yarrow was tough to pick too ("Who

drinks yarrow tea?"). White and yellow bedstraw and the ground cover of kingfingers were easily identified. Honeysuckle, rare in the Vale, scrambled happily over thorn bushes, with gorse also mingled. Wild clematis, called "Old Man's Beard", climbed up last year's dead wood. There were also shrubs which had the strange name of guelder roses. Sometimes, leaves of wild peppermint could be crushed and tasted; sometimes, the leaves of sorrel were bitten.

To penetrate into the shade of the oak scrub and then into the taller beechwoods was to encounter wild garlic ("rub it and smell it") and the rather dreary dog's mercury, which did not seem to merit such an interesting name. The woods were, in fact, rather frightening, but there was the attraction that in the loose earth round the tree trunks, it was possible to find flints. Those in which there were holes were especially sought-after. To strike two flints together might even produce smoke – and a sulphurous smell.

The climax of the Wendover walk was The Monument, commemorating something called The Boer War. Somehow, it seemed out place on such a spot. Rather than climb up its steps it was more interesting to look at the panorama of the Vale and to pick out familiar landmarks or to contemplate the smooth grassy flanks of what was popularly known as "Velvet Lawn" rather than Cymbeline's Mount. Below it was Ellesborough church where, on one occasion, a cottage was visited where a man was drawing water from a deep well. It was fed from a chalk spring and was very cold.

Another way to travel to "The Hills" was on one of the omnibuses which ran on an uncertain schedule to Princes Risborough. To sit on the open top deck was an exciting experience. It was necessary to duck to avoid the branches which at intervals were almost low enough to strike the vehicles. A drive was once made in a neighbour's car to the same area, but it finished in the vicinity of Terrick crossroads. An explosion resulting from a puncture and a sagging of the back part of the vehicle caused a great deal of annoyance and distress – everybody out and standing embarrassed on the side of the road while the wheel was changed.

It was the first time that such an event had been experienced. Back in the car, rugs were put over the knees (though it was summer time) and fond hopes were expressed that it would not happen again.

The road to Terrick passed through Stoke Mandeville, the earliest memory of which is a row of *Lilium candidum* ("The Madonna lily") alongside a brick path in a friend's garden. Their heady scent and dusty yellow pollen immediately attracted attention and permission was given to pick several. Unfortunately it was assumed that picking consisted of removing the flowers and leaving behind a row of beheaded stems.

In the Hills there was also a place called Tring, but it was regarded as foreign because it was not in Buckinghamshire. Tring road was a long straight road which opened up a panorama of hills beyond Broughton turn. It was reputed to be a Roman road. Tring was the home of one of the several members of the Rothschild family. There were no castles in the Vale of Aylesbury, but there were mansions and the most impressive of them were built by the Rothschild family. The villages in which they had located their mansions acquired a special character, "Rothschild houses", architect-designed with a carved coat-of-arms, were built for the retaining staff. Many farms were also purchased by the Rothschilds in the Vale. Those who farmed them were called "Rothschild tenants". It was said that they had "to do what they were told"; but it was known that they shared in the product of "shooting parties" and were recipients of coveted Christmas presents. The small town of Tring benefitted from the presence in its centre of the Rothschild mansion. There was nothing like it in Aylesbury and it was occupied by a Lord.

Among the inhabitants of the Vale of Aylesbury, Rothschild was a name which breathed all that stood for wealth. "To behave as though he or she was a Rothschild" was a characteristic ascribed to anyone who (in the eyes of others) was living extravagantly. "Anyone would think that they were Rothschilds" was an unflattering term applied to any in the circle of acquaintances who had acquired something deemed to be an unnecessary luxury. In Tring, it was the natural history museum of Lord Rothschild that was the object of a visit to the town. The stuffed animals and birds never had much appeal, but the display cabinet containing the butterfly collections were irresistible. A special source of interest was a glass case in which the day-by-day development of an egg into a chicken was displayed. It was probably instrumental in generating a distaste for eggs, especially boiled eggs. Tring was mentally associated with something called The Tring and District Draghounds. They were regarded as peculiar and as inferior to The Whaddon Chase Foxhounds. The Drag Hunt was described as following the scent of a trail left by a man dragging a sack of aniseed. It all seemed very improbable. By inference, it might have caused a personal distaste for a popular schoolboy sweet – aniseed balls.

Near to the top of Tring Hill, in an abandoned chalk quarry was a railway carriage with a smoky chimney pipe which had been converted into some sort of dwelling. It was a story-tale house. From the summit of the hill, glimpses could be seen of "The Reservoirs": these were described as "man-made lakes" to provide a supply of water to the local canals. In the vicinity of Tring Hill were also to be found the Chiltern Springs, from which the district's water supply derived. The pumping station was near a place with the unlikely name of Dancer's End. From Tring Hill it was possible to see Dunstable Downs ("Why are they Dunstable Downs and not Hills?" One asked. "Why are they Wendover Hills and not Downs?").

Just occasionally, there were evening trips in summer in a neighbour's car to Ashridge or Hampden Common. Both seemed exotic places. It was a source of disappointment not being allowed to go to the top the Bridgewater monument ("It isn't safe for children . . . You'll get giddy going round the spiral staircase"). To see the occasional deer, head held high above the acres of bracken, was a bonus at Ashridge. The bonus at Hampden usually came in the form of an effervescent drink at the public house on the common.

Such outings were only for the handful of people who had cars. Summer holidays were experienced by even fewer and of those who had cars, few risked driving them to the sea. It was said that

Aylesbury was about as far from the coast as any place in England. To reach the sea called for an exciting journey by train – possibly two trains.

Sea and sand were what were sought – and sun, it was hoped. Once on the sands, the immediate prospect was somewhat frightening. It took some time to adjust to the mass of water called the sea. It appeared to go on for ever, though it was usually possible to distinguish the thin line that marked the boundary between sea and sky. For optical reasons, the line seemed to be disarmingly higher than the beach on which one played. In addition, there was the mysterious tide. Why did it stop coming in or stop going out?

The sea was always cold. Even on hot days there was a sneaking wind which wrapped round the body. There were hard pebbles which bruised soft feet. The waves broke disturbingly. Sometimes there were jellyfish to be avoided. It was not like trying to swim in Aylesbury baths.

The rock pools were a source of much attraction, with their seaweeds, shells and small crustaceans.[18] The sea-edge smells appealed, though they were probably those of decaying vegetation. For want of a better word they were declared to be those of "the ozone". The sound of seagulls haunted, though they behaved less

Fig. 21. The author, left, with his brother, right.

agreeably to each other than the so-called "land gulls" that followed the plough in Buckinghamshire.

Strands of seaweed were brought home annually. They were hung up and sniffed from time to time with the eyes closed. They were supposed to bring back seaside sensations. It was comforting to open the eyes on the familiar intimate landscapes of the Vale of Aylesbury and not on the endless water of the ocean.

XI

"THE HUGE COURT OF THE MEMORY"

The epithet of St Augustin may appear to be rather grand to apply to such a simple document as this, but it calls to mind the infinite detail, especially from early days, that is stored in the memory bank. The sights, sounds, smells and feelings and the ways in which they are linked together are highly personal. The associations that stir them are even more so. Yet, given expression, many of them immediately strike sympathetic chords in others. There is no denying that walking the streets, roads, lanes and footpaths, with time to stand and stare and question was a childhood education no less important than that received formally in school. Such quotidian experiences were widely shared two generations ago and must, for that reason, account for the minute particulars that can be remembered by so many.

The Swiss educationalist J.H. Pestalozzi believed that the education of the young should begin with a knowledge of the place in which they lived and that the process should gradually extend into the countryside and the wider world beyond. In the 1920s, Aylesbury, being small enough to be covered on foot, could be appreciated as a whole. For a child, it acquired an identity of its own, with the encompassing Vale generating its own sense of locality. As acquaintance grew, the town and its surroundings became a little *patrie* in the best French sense of the word, fostering almost unconsciously a local patriotism. There is plenty of evidence, all too little of it committed to paper, to suggest that the experience was not uncommon.

NOTES

1. Following the death of my mother during the Spanish 'flu epidemic in 1918, my six month old brother was taken care of in the children's ward of the Royal Bucks Hospital and I was sent to be looked after by an uncle and aunt at Aston Abbots. Little can be recalled of these events. It is probably hearsay that I travelled there on a carrier's cart – though I do remember (probably later) sitting with others on a carrier's cart which came twice weekly to Aylesbury market. (From Wingrave via Aston Abbots?) The original journey was more likely to have been in a pony and trap.

   The eventual return to Aylesbury was to a home where a housekeeper had been installed. Jenny (Jane Eliza) King had been a nursemaid to my father and his younger brother when his own mother had died. Jenny came from a large family in Stewkley. In all senses of the word she exuded Victorian values and practices. She was a stalwart of the Wesleyan chapel in Buckingham Street, became very much a *mater familias* and a genuine Buckingham Street character to all and sundry during the twenty years that she lived there.

2. William Rutland Boughton, the composer, suffered from the straitened circumstances of the family when the business failed. Benefactors in Aylesbury helped with his musical education. In the 1920s he had a phenomenal success with his opera *The Immortal Hour*. No opera in London has beaten the number of performances on successive nights. (cf Michael Hurd, *Rutland Boughton and the Glastonbury Festival*, OUP, 1993). In the company of Arthur Tattersall, Secretary of UCL, paths crossed with its star, Gwen Ffrangcon-Davies some forty years later. In the 1930s Rutland Boughton had close connections with Charles Pope, music master at Aylesbury Grammar School and visited his old school on a number of occasions. A blue plaque on the first floor of No 37 Buckingham Street, placed there by the Aylesbury Society, commemorates his association with the building. (It is best seen from the top of a double-decker bus).

3. In the 1920s the household consisted of my father, uncle, the housekeeper, the housemaid, two shop assistants (occasionally three), a variable number of so-called errand boys (from two to four). There always seemed to be much toing-and-froing of people – in and out of the side door and warehouse doors in Cambridge Place. There came a steady stream of delivery men and salesmen, dustmen, coalmen, postmen, window cleaners, handymen, milkmen, papermen and an anonymous woman who called on Friday evenings for the washing. By and large it was a fairly representative Aylesbury family business, replicated all round the town. As was still the practice at the time, William and Leopold Mead served formal apprenticeships – at the end of which they received formal legal documents. They were apprenticed to a cousin in Leighton Buzzard who was a corn

chandler as well as a "Master" grocer and provision merchant.

4. Many years later, the geological memoir covering North Bucks and Oxfordshire confirmed the fact.

5. Mary's widowed mother arranged the marriage to John Wilkes, who subsequently divorced her and disposed of The Prebendal. See Arthur H. Cash, John Wilkes, *The Scandalous Father of Civil Liberty*, Yale University Press, 2006. The story of *The Prebendal* is told by Hugh Hanley (1983).

6. In fact, the Gilbert & Sullivan Opera group gave its first performance in 1930 – the beginning of what was to become ADOS (Aylesbury Dramatic & Opera Society) and to enjoy an honourable life of well over seventy years. (Kenneth Evans, its oral historian – indeed its archivist with his collection of programmes and posters).

7. Interesting to learn via the Fairground Archive of the University of Sheffield, that the outermost horses "galloped" at 20 mph and that quantities of real gold leaf were lavished on their decoration.

8. It was not surprising that botany should appeal because there was already an interest in plants and the cultivation of a personal garden patch. A daily diary from 1928 records that it was a common practice in summer to get up an hour earlier to attend to it before going to school. The 1929 diary from the time records the pocket money spent on seeds, plants and bulbs. It also included a page of what would now be called phenological records. At the time, flowers were also being pressed and dried. There is a distinct memory of pressed harebells retaining their blue colour and being made into a montage for a birthday card. Pressed flowers were also stuck into autograph albums which were in fashion at the time. At a later stage, the contents of the herbarium at the County Museum were much admired.

9. *Caltha palustris* was first associated with the lake at Hartwell. It was amusing to learn later that it had 60 common names in France, 80 in Britain and at least 140 in Germany, Austria and Switzerland (Pavord, op. cit., p397). Also that Leonardo da Vinci made a drawing of it.

10. *The Naming of Names*, by Anna Pavord (2007) gave a new depth of appreciation to "the naming of the parts" (apologies to Philip Larkin) of flowers. It began around 300 BC with those simple monosyllabic words – leaf, stem, bud, seed. Later came the disyllabic – petal, sepal, stamen. And how it would have thrilled our botany master to read the description of a single weed in the *Herbal* of William Turner – the dead nettle (Pavord p267) – and to know that John Ray was the first author to use the word "botany". Richard Fortey, *The Secret Life of the Natural History Museum* (2008) was also encountered at the same time with its chapter on "Theatre of Plants", pp 156–187.

11. In the inter-war years the school published an annual magazine *The Aylesburian*. Its articles include many items about life in the school at the time. There are also recollections included in W. R. Mead, *Aylesbury Grammar School 1598–1998* (1995).

The portrait was an original from the late sixteenth century. It was given to the school in the 1890s by a member of the Lee family. It was destroyed in the fire of 1953. With the substantial sum received from the insurance a copy was made of the Henry Lee portrait in the Tudor Room of The National Gallery.

12. Quarrendon has a special place personally. The ruins of the mediaeval church, covered by brambles and wild rose were a picnic site and the object of several childhood visits. The site of the lost village was visited in the company of Maurice Beresford at the time that he was writing *The Lost Villages of England* (1954). It was also the time when one of the Terry family's retired hunters was occasionally ridden over all the Quarrendon land and also to Church Farm at Aston Abbots via Weedon. In 1998, on the occasion of the 400th anniversary of the foundation of Aylesbury Grammar School a commemorative service was held on the site of the chapel where Sir Henry Lee was buried. Paul Everson's impressive study of Quarrendon, *Records of Buckinghamshire*, 41, 2001 and reprinted as Peasants, Peer and Graziers, The Landscape of Quarrendon, *Buckinghamshire Papers*, 9, 2006 was enjoyed with much pleasure. Following a memorable "Open Day" in 2006 and in conjunction with the Berryfields housing development, 83 hectares of land covering the historic Quarrendon sites had been transferred to a Buckinghamshire Conservation Trust.

13. Hartwell House was seen annually as the backdrop to the County Agricultural Show. It also acquired a personal connection through the last private owner, Dr John Lee (cf. W. R. Mead, Dr John Lee of Hartwell and his Swedish Journey 1507–1509, *Records of Buckinghamshire* (2003), 43, 9–26). Hugh Hanley, *Hartwell House* (1986) has been out of print far too long. Hartwell has also inspired the definitive publications of Eric Throssell beginning with *The Triumphal Arch* (The Long Gallery Press, 2007).

14. No one seems to have paid attention to the fact that Manor House was the boyhood home of Sir Henry Layard, MP for Aylesbury (1852–6), which he thought "a dull country town". Sir Henry Layard was a pioneering archaeologist who discovered the site of Nineveh and who is remembered in the suite of Assyrian rooms at the British Museum, attracted personal attention because of an unpublished diary covering his journey through Finland on his way to St Petersburg in 1838.

15. The Stewkley roots of the Mead family are to be found in W. R. Mead, *Adopting Finland* (Helsinki, 2007) 144–5. See also Henry Mead, *William Mead, Quaker and his Relations* (London, 1918). Thomas Hardy's poem "The Family Face" provides appropriate words:

> I am the family face
> Flesh perishes, I live on
> Projecting trait and trace
> Through time to times anon.

16. Many years later, a reference was made to the experience (Ridge and Furrow in Buckinghamshire, *Geographical Journal*, 1953).

17. It never seemed possible to remember more than a couple of consecutive

lines of verse. In addition to the R. L. Stevenson couplet, another regularly recalled from school days is Rudyard Kipling's "Serving Men". Their names are

> What and why and when
> And how and where and who.

Thomas Hood's "November" also stuck (or at least part of it)

> No sun, no moon
> No morn, no noon,
> No dawn, no dusk
> No proper time of day

and so on to. . .

> November.

18. All the feelings came back when reading L. P. Hartley, *The Shrimp and the Anemone* (1944). The last pages had a considerable impact. It was an unexpected privilege to sit next to L. P. Hartley at a British Council lunch and to ask him if it took him three hours, three weeks or three months to write the final few pages.

Gardening
CASH ACCOUNT

Gardening
CASH ACCOUNT

Date.	Particulars.	Received. COST.	Paid.	Date.	Particulars.	Received. COST.	Paid.
		£ s d	£ s d		Brought forward	£ s d	£ s d
Feb 4	Laburnam	1 6	1 6			17 0	17 0
6	Rose Tree (R.T.)	1 3	2 9	June 1	1 Rock Plant	6	17 6
		2 0	2 0	8	Marigold.	6	18 0
Mar 25	Fork & Trowel	1 0	3 0	14	Plant & Labels	6	18 6
26	Seeds (Mignonette)	2	3 11	21	Kaleanthums	6	19 0
27	Do. (Poppys & Marigold)	2	4 1	29	Creepers & Bushes	1 3	0 3
30	6 Locks? (Ajulica)	1 0	5 1				1 0 9
		2 4	5 1	July 6	Rock Plant	6	1 0 9
Apr 6	8 Saxifrages, thrift etc	1 6	6 7	27	Trellis work	4 0	1 4 9
10	3 Columbines, 1 Geum	1 0	7 7	29	Arch (Trellis)	5 6	1 10 3
13	Narcissi etc. J.H.	6	8 1	29	Poles	9	1 11 0
15	Do	4	8 5	31	Antirrhinums	1	1 11 4
17	6 Pansies, R. Lavender	1 6	10 1			1 11 4	
20	6 Pansies, 1 Polyanthus	1 4	11 5	Aug 1	Stakes	9	1 12 1
30	Hoe	8	12 1	3	Antirrhinums	4	1 12 4
20	1 Polyanthus Red	3	12 4	24	Wallflowers, Sweet	1 6	1 13 0
27	2 Anemones & daleas	1 0	13 4		Williams, Forget-	1 6	1 15 4
		8 1	13 4		me-nots	1 6	1 16 10
May 4	4 pansies, J.E.B.	1 0	14 4			5 1	1 16 1
6	"Plant-tie"	4	14 8	Sep 14	Hanging Basket	6	1 17 1
11	6 Pinks, 6 Nemesi	8	15 4	14	Trowel (Hand)	6	1 17 1
14	2 Sweet Williams	4	15 8	16	18 Tulips 2 Hya.	2 0	1 19 1
18	S.W. 6 Gaillardias	10	16 6			3 0	1 19 1
25	1 Geranium	6	17 0	Oct 4	8 Daffodils	1 0	2 0 1
		5 8			Carried ford.	1 0	2 0 1
	Brought forward		17 0				

Fig. 22. By schooldays there was already a keen interest in a personal garden plot. As the dia[ry]
from 1928–9 records, it was a regular practice to get up an hour earlier in the summer to atte[nd]
to it before going to school. All pocket money was spent on plants, seeds and bulbs. A "Natu[re]
memorandum" supplemented the school diary of 1928–9.

Dodecatheon meadia *flore albo.*

Fig. 23. Dodecatheon meadia

Richard Mead (1673–1754) is of personal interest not because he was the first major medical authority on scurvy, as is evident from the publications in the British Library Catalogue, but because of his botanical interests. Carl Linnaeus named a plant after him – *Dodecatheon media flore albo*, by G. Loddiges, first published in *Loddiges Botanical Cabinet*, plate 1489, Vol XV, 1828. (Reproduced with the kind permission of the Director and the Board of Trustees, Royal Botanic Gardens, Kew). Perhaps it should be the floral symbol of the Mead family at large.

The family tree has never been investigated, but the Stewkley roots of the Mead family at large are well documented. In addition the Williams and Richards recur from generation to generation. (See Henry Mead, *William Mead, Quaker and his Relations*, London 1918.)

Generation No. 1
William Mead was born 1548, Stewkley, Bucks.
William's grandfather is probably Richard Mead, church warden of Soulbury in 1523.
Children of Richard Mead are:
– William Mead, b. 1580, Stewkley, Bucks.
– Richard Mead, b. 1583, Stewkley, Bucks.

Generation No. 2
Richard Mead was born 1583, Stewkley, Bucks.; married Elizabeth Hawes 1604.
Child of Richard Mead and Elizabeth ? is:
– Richard Mead, b.ca. 1605, Bragenham, Soulbury, Bucks.; d. 1643, Soulbury, Bucks.

Generation No. 3
Richard Mead was born ca. 1605, Bragenham, Soulbury, Bucks.; died 1643, Soulbury, Bucks.
He married *Joane ?*.
Children of Richard Mead and Joane ? are:
– Richard Mead, b.1626, Soulbury, Bucks., d. 1690, Mursley, Bucks.
– William, Mead, b. 1627 Soulbury, Bucks., d. 1713, Goosehays, Romford, Essex; One of his daughters was Mrs. Phillips, mother of Henry Phillips who created the Aylesbury Grammar School Foundation.
– Mathew Mead, b. 1629, Soulbury, Bucks.
– Thomas Mead, b. 1632, Soulbury, Bucks.
– Elizabeth Mead, b. 1633, Soulbury, Bucks.
– John Mead, b. 1634, Soulbury, Bucks.
– Samuel Mead, b. 1635, Soulbury, Bucks.
– Rebecca Mead, b. 1637, Soulbury, Bucks.
– Joane Mead, b. 1639, Soulbury, Bucks.
– Sarah Mead, b. 1641, Soulbury, Bucks.

Generation No. 4
Richard Mead born 1626, Soulbury, Bucks.; died 1690, Mursley, Bucks. He married *Joane ?*
Children of Richard Mead and Joane ? are:
– John Mead, b.ca. 1660. John Mead was a wealthy drysalter in London. He owned the manor of Tottenhoe in Bedfordshire.
– Joane Mead, b.ca. 1661
– Francis Mead, b. 1663; d. 1732, Aylesbury
– Robert Mead, b.ca. 1665; died 1725, Aylesbury. He married Ann ?
– Sarah Mead, b.ca. 1667
– Rebecca Mead, b.ca. 1670
William Mead, born ca. 1670; died 1723, Soulbury, Bucks. He was High Sheriff of Buckinghamshire in 1716. Buried at Soulbury. (See History of Aylesbury Grammar School).